IIASA PROCEEDINGS SERIES

Volume 3

Nonsmooth Optimization

IIASA PROCEEDINGS SERIES

NOTICE TO READERS

Dear Reader

If your library is not already a standing order customer or subscriber to this series, may we recommend that you place a standing or subscription order to receive immediately upon publication all new issues and volumes published in this valuable series. Should you find that these volumes no longer serve your needs your order can be cancelled at any time without notice.

ROBERT MAXWELL
Publisher at Pergamon Press

NONSMOOTH OPTIMIZATION

Proceedings of a IIASA Workshop,
March 28 - April 8, 1977

CLAUDE LEMARECHAL
ROBERT MIFFLIN
Editors

PERGAMON PRESS

OXFORD · NEW YORK · TORONTO · SYDNEY · PARIS · FRANKFURT

U.K.	Pergamon Press Ltd., Headington Hill Hall, Oxford OX3 0BW, England
U.S.A.	Pergamon Press Inc., Maxwell House, Fairview Park, Elmsford, New York 10523, U.S.A.
CANADA	Pergamon of Canada, Suite 104, 150 Consumers Road, Willowdale, Ontario M2 J1P9, Canada
AUSTRALIA	Pergamon Press (Aust.) Pty. Ltd., 19a Boundary Street, Rushcutters Bay, N.S.W. 2011, Australia
FRANCE	Pergamon Press SARL, 24 rue des Ecoles, 75240 Paris, Cedex 05, France
FEDERAL REPUBLIC OF GERMANY	Pergamon Press GmbH, 6242 Kronberg-Taunus, Pferdstrasse 1, Federal Republic of Germany

British Library Cataloguing in Publication Data

Nonsmooth optimization. - (International Institute for Applied Systems Analysis.
IIASA proceedings series; Vol. 3).
1. System analysis - Congresses
2. Mathematical optimization - Congresses
I. Lemarechal, Claude II. Mifflin, Robert
III. Series
003   QA402   78-40904
ISBN 0-08-023428-3

*Printed in Great Britain by
William Clowes & Sons Limited
Beccles and London*

PREFACE

Task 2 of the System and Decision Sciences Area, Optimization, is a central methodological tool of systems analysis. It is used and needed by many Tasks at IIASA, including those of the Energy Systems and the Food and Agriculture Programs. In order to deal with large-scale applications by means of decomposition techniques, it is necessary to be able to optimize functions that are not differentiable everywhere. This is the concern of the subtask Nonsmooth Optimization. Methods of nonsmooth optimization have been applied to a model for determining equilibrium prices for agricultural commodities in world trade. They are also readily applicable to some other IIASA models on allocating resources in health care systems.

This volume is the result of a workshop on Nonsmooth Optimization that met at IIASA in the Spring of 1977. It consists of papers on the techniques and theory of nonsmooth optimization, a set of numerical test problems for future experimentation, and a comprehensive research bibliography.

CONTENTS

INTRODUCTION

This volume is the result of a workshop on nonsmooth optimization held at IIASA from March 28 to April 8, 1977. The designation "First World Conference on Nonsmooth Optimization", proposed in jest by one of the participants after noting that there were only nine others in the room with him, is, however, appropriate because of the various countries represented, and because the number of scientists doing research in this field at that time was rather small.

The small number of participants, and the workshop's unusual length, made it possible to achieve a substantial exchange of information. Each morning (three working hours) was devoted to the talk of one participant, who therefore could present his work quite thoroughly. During the afternoons, discussions took place on related topics, such as: systems of inequalities, constrained problems, test problems and numerical experiments, smooth approximation of nonsmooth functions, optimization with noise, direction-finding procedures and quadratic programming, line searches, general decomposition, ... However, this workshop format would have been a failure were it not for the fact that everyone was alert and active even when not "in the spotlight". We are very grateful to all the participants, who contributed to the success of the workshop by their numerous questions and interruptions during both the formal and informal presentations.

This workshop was held under the name Nondifferentiable Optimization, but it has been recognized that this is misleading, because it suggests "optimization without derivatives". As we view it, nonsmooth optimization (NSO) is concerned with problems having functions for which gradients exist almost everywhere, but are not continuous, so that the usual gradient-based methods and results fail. The contents of these Proceedings should convince the reader of the importance of being able to compute (generalized) gradients in NSO.

We have adopted the following topical classification for the papers: subgradient optimization (three papers), descent methods (four papers), and field of applicability (one paper).

The first paper, by B.T. Poljak, exhaustively surveys the Soviet work on subgradient optimization done since 1962. For this method he gives the

1

most important results obtained and the various extensions that have been developed.

J.L. Goffin studies rates of convergence in subgradient optimization. He shows under which conditions linear convergence can be obtained and provides bounds on the best possible rate of convergence. These bounds are given in terms of condition numbers that do not depend on derivative continuity.

The paper by R. Chaney and A.A. Goldstein addresses the question: What is the most general framework for the method of subgradient optimization to be applicable and convergent? Hence, they present the method in an abstract setting and study the minimal hypotheses required to ensure convergence.

One of the important conclusions of this workshop has been that nonsmooth optimization and nonlinear programming (NLP) are, in fact, equivalent fields. It was known that NLP is contained in NSO via exact penalty function methods, but B.N. Pshenichnyi's paper demonstrates the reverse containment via feasible direction methods.

In his paper, C. Lemarechal describes, in a unified setting, descent methods developed recently in Western countries. He also provides ideas for improvement of these methods.

Many methods for solving constrained optimization problems require the repeated solution of constrained least squares problems for search direction determination. An efficient and reliable algorithm for solving such subproblems is given in the paper by R. Mifflin.

The paper by P. Wolfe is concerned with line searches. He gives an APL algorithm that effectively deals with the issues of when to stop a line search with a satisfactory step size and how to determine the next trial step size when the stopping criterion is not met.

The last paper, by J. Gauvin, studies the differential properties of extremal value functions. This is important for the application of various decomposition schemes for solving large-scale optimization problems, because these approaches require the solution of nonsmooth problems involving extremal-value functions, and in order to guarantee convergence we need to know whether certain "semismoothness" conditions (such as Lipschitz continuity) are satisfied.

We then give four nonsmooth optimization test problems. They were selected because they are easy to work with and because they are representative both of the field of applicability and of the range of difficulty of

NSO. Problems 1 and 3 are examples of minimax problems and are not very difficult. Problem 2 is a nonconvex problem coming from a well-known NLP test problem, and problem 4 involves a piecewise-linear function. The last two are sufficiently difficult to slow down considerably the speed of convergence of any of the NSO methods we know of.

We conclude this volume with a large NSO bibliography. It was compiled by the participants and is an update of the bibliography given in *Mathematical Programming Study 3*. We wish to thank D.P. Bertsekas, V.F. Demjanov, M.L. Fisher, and E.A. Nurminskii for the items they communicated to us.

On behalf of all the participants we would like to acknowledge IIASA's generous support and to thank I. Beckey, L. Berg, A. Fildes, and G. Lindelof for their optimal organizational contributions, which led to a smooth-running workshop.

We are especially indebted to M.L. Balinski who was instrumental in establishing a Nonsmooth Optimization group at IIASA and who spent much of his time and energy to secure a truly international participation at this workshop.

C. Lemarechal
R. Mifflin

SUBGRADIENT METHODS:
A SURVEY OF SOVIET RESEARCH

B. T. Poljak

This paper reviews research efforts by Soviet authors concerning the subgradient technique of nondifferentiable minimization and its extensions. It does not cover the works based on the concept of steepest descent (by V.F. Demjanov, B.N. Pshenichnyi, E.S. Levitin, and others) or on the use of a specific form of the minimizing function (for example minimax techniques). The paper essentially uses the review by N.Z. Shor [1]. The theorems given below are mostly simplified versions of results shown in the original papers.

1. THE SUBGRADIENT METHOD

Let $f(x)$ be a convex continuous function in the space R^n. A vector $\partial f(x) \in R^n$ is called its subgradient at the point x, if it satisfies the condition

$$f(x+y) \geq f(x) + (\partial f(x), y) \quad , \quad \forall y \in R^n \quad . \tag{1}$$

A subgradient exists (although, generally speaking, it may be not unique) for all $x \in R^n$. If $f(x)$ is differentiable, the subgradient is unique and coincides with the gradient $\partial f(x) = \nabla f(x)$. The rules of subgradient calculation for various types of functions are well known [2,3]. In particular, with $f(x) = \max_{1 \leq i \leq m} f_i(x)$ where $f_i(x)$ are convex differentiable functions, it is true that

$$\partial f(x) = \sum_{i \in I(x)} \alpha_i \nabla f_i(x) \quad , \quad \alpha_i \geq 0 \quad ,$$

$$\sum_{i \in I(x)} \alpha_i = 1 \quad , \quad I(x) = \{i : f_i(x) = f(x)\}$$

5

(for instance one may take $\partial f(x) = \nabla f_i(x)$ where $i \in I(x)$ is arbitrary).

The subgradient minimization method for $f(x)$ on R^n is an iterative process of the form

$$x_{k+1} = x_k - \gamma_k \partial f(x_k) / \| \partial f(x_k) \| \qquad (2)$$

where $\gamma_k \geq 0$ is a step size. For differentiable functions this method coincides with the gradient one. The major difference between the gradient and the subgradient methods is that, generally speaking, the direction $-\partial f(x_k)$ is not a descent direction at the point x_k; i.e., the values of $f(x_k)$ for nondifferentiable functions do not decrease monotonically in the method (2).

The subgradient method was developed in 1962 by N.Z. Shor and used by him for solving large-scale transportation problems of linear programming [4]. Although published in a low-circulation publication, this pioneering work became widely known to experts in the optimization area in the USSR. Also of great importance for the propagation of nondifferentiable optimization concepts were the reports by the same author presented in a number of conferences in 1962-1966.

Publication of papers [5,6,7] giving a precise statement of the method and its convergence theorems may be regarded as the culmination of the first stage in developing subgradient techniques.

Let us get down to describing the basic results concerning the subgradient method. As is known, the gradient method for minimization of smooth functions employs the following ways to regulate the step-size:

$$\gamma_k = \alpha \| \partial f(x_k) \| \quad ,$$

i.e.

$$x_{k+1} = x_k - \alpha \nabla f(x_k) \quad , \qquad 0 < \alpha < \bar{\alpha}$$

(the ordinary gradient method);

$$\gamma_k = \arg \min_{\gamma} f(x_k - \gamma \partial f(x_k) / \| \partial f(x_k) \|)^{\dagger}$$

(the steepest descent method).

Simple examples may be constructed to show that neither of these methods converges in nondifferentiable minimization; this necessitates the construction of new principles of selecting the step size. Consider the major ones. Hereinafter we shall assume $f(x)$ to be convex and continuous and denote $f^* = \inf f(x)$ and $X^* = \text{Arg min } f(x)$.

(a) $\gamma_k = \gamma > 0$. This constant-step method was suggested in [4]. The simplest example, $f(x) = |x|$, $x \in R^1$, explicitly proves that this method does not converge. One may show, however, that it gives a solution "with an accuracy of γ".

Theorem 1 [4]

Let X^* be nonempty. Then for any $\delta > 0$ there exists $\bar{\gamma} > 0$ such that in the method (2) with $\gamma_k = \gamma$, $0 < \gamma < \bar{\gamma}$ we have $\lim \inf f(x_k) < f^* + \delta$.

Reference [4] has described the following way of step-size regulation resting upon this result, although it has not been entirely formalized. A certain $\gamma > 0$ is chosen and the computation is made with $\gamma_k = \gamma$ until the values of $f(x_k)$ start to oscillate about a certain limit. After this γ is halved and the process is repeated.

(b) The sequence γ_k is chosen a priori regardless of the computation results and satisfies the condition

$$\sum_{k=0}^{\infty} \gamma_k = \infty , \qquad \gamma_k \to 0 . \qquad (3)$$

This way of choosing the step-size has been suggested in [5] and [6] independently.

---

†Hereafter arg min $\rho(\gamma)$ will mean an arbitrary minimum point of
 the function $\rho(\gamma)$, Arg min $\rho(\gamma)$ is the set of all minimum points.

Theorem 2 [5,6]

In the method (2),(3) lim inf $f(x_k) = f^*$. If X* is nonempty and bounded then $\rho(x_k,X^*) \to 0$, where

$$\rho(x,X^*) = \min_{x^* \varepsilon X^*} \| x - x^* \| \quad .$$

It is clear that in the general case the method (2),(3) cannot converge faster than γ_k tends to zero. In particular, this method never converges at the rate of geometrical progression or at the rate

$$O(k^{-s}), \quad s > 1 \quad .$$

(c) In certain cases the value of f* is known. For instance, if

$$f(x) = \sum_{i=1}^{m} f_i(x)_+ \quad ,$$

where $f_i(x)$ are convex functions,

$$f_i(x)_t = \max \{0, f_i(x)\} \quad ,$$

and the system of inequalities $f_i(x) \le 0$ i = 1,...,m is solvable, then X* is the set of solutions of this system and f* = 0. Then one may take

$$\gamma_k = \lambda \frac{(f(x_k) - f^*)}{\| \partial f(x_k) \|} \quad , \quad 0 < \lambda < 2 \quad . \tag{4}$$

In solving systems of inequalities the method (3),(4) coincides with the known relaxation method of Kaczmarz, Agmon, Motzkin, Schoenberg, and Eremin [8]. The method for general problems of nonsmooth function minimization has in essence been suggested by I.I. Eremin [9] and systematically developed in [10].

Theorem 3 [9,10]

Let x* be the unique minimum point for f(x). Then in the method (2),(4) $x_k \rightarrow x^*$. If the condition

$$f(x) - f^* \geq \ell \|x - x^*\| \quad , \quad \ell > 0 \tag{5}$$

holds, the method converges with the rate of a geometrical progression.

The advantages of the method (2),(4) are the simplicity of selecting the step size (since no auxiliary problems should be solved and no characteristics of f(x) other than f* should be known) and its applicability, since for a smooth strongly convex f(x) the method also converges with the rate of a geometrical progression [10]. Reference [10] has shown a way to modify the technique when f* is unknown.

(d) N.Z. Shor [11] has suggested an essentially different method for choosing γ_k:

$$\gamma_k = \gamma_0 q^k \quad , \quad 0 < q < 1 \quad . \tag{6}$$

Note that the condition (3) is not satisfied for (6).

Theorem 4 [11,12,13]

Let the condition

$$(\partial f(x), x - x^*) \geq \ell \|\partial f(x)\| \; \|x - x^*\| \quad , \quad \ell > 0 \tag{7}$$

hold. Then there exists a pair $\bar{q}$ (which depends on ℓ) and $\bar{\gamma}$ (which depends on $\|x_0 - x^*\|$, ℓ) such that with $1 > q \geq \bar{q}$, $\gamma_0 \geq \bar{\gamma}$ in the method (2),(6) we have

$$\|x_k - x^*\| \leq C(q, \gamma_0) q^k \quad .$$

The relationship of $\bar{q}(\ell)$ and $\bar{\gamma}(\|x_0 - x^*\|, \ell)$ may be expressed explicitly. However, practical implementation of the method (2),(6) faces difficulties because generally the values of ℓ and $\| x_0 - x^* \|$ are unknown.

The above results prove that the convergence rate for any of the step-size regulating rules is linear at best. The denominator of the geometrical progression for the ill-conditioned problems (i.e. for functions with greatly extended level sets) is near unity. Thus the convergence rate of all the versions of the subgradient method may be rather poor.

2. ACCELERATING CONVERGENCE OF THE SUBGRADIENT METHOD

One of the reasons why the subgradient method converges so slowly lies in its Markov nature. The subsequent iteration makes no use of the information obtained at the previous steps. The major concept of all techniques for accelerating convergence is the use of this information (i.e. the values $f(x_i)$, $\partial f(x_i)$, $i=0,\ldots,k-1$).

The first methods of this type were those developed by Kelley and by Cheney and Goldstein [14,15], based on piecewise-linear approximation of the function. An original technique suggested in [16] and [17] independently made use only of the values $\partial f(x_i)$. Let M_k be a polyhedron in R^n in which the minimum point is localized after k iterations. Then for an arbitrary $x_{k+1} \in M_k$ one may take

$$M_{k+1} = M_k \cap \{x: (\partial f(x_{k+1}), x - x_{k+1}) \leq 0\} \ .$$

If the center of gravity M_k is taken as the point x_{k+1} one may show [17] that for the volume V_k of the polyhedron M_k the following expression holds:

$$V_{k+1} \leq [1-(1 - \frac{1}{N-1})^N]V_k \ ,$$

where N is the dimension of the space. Thus for problems of any dimension

$$V_k \leq V_0 q^k \ , \quad q = 1 - e^{-1} \ .$$

In other words, the method converges with the rate of geometrical progression, the denominator being independent of both the properties of the function and the dimension of the space. This result is mostly of theoretical interest since the auxiliary problem of finding the center of gravity for the polyhedron is very difficult to solve. References [17,18,19] give a number of modified techniques in which a simpler auxiliary problem is solved at each step. References [18,19] have also shown that the center-of-gravity technique is optimal in a certain sense. Roughly speaking, there is no algorithm that uses the same information and provides better convergence. A similar result for algorithms that uses only the values $f(x_i)$ rather than $\partial f(x_i)$ is given in Reference [20].

These methods [14,15,16,17,18,19,20] have been developed independently of the subgradient method. Let us turn now to the algorithms obtained as a direct extension of (2).

Let the value of f* be known. Reference [10] suggests the following technique. At the kth step the quadratic programming problem is solved:

$$\min \| x - x_k \|^2$$

$$f(x_k) + (\partial f(x_k),\ x - x_k) \le f*$$

$$f(x_{k-1}) + (\partial f(x_{k-1}), x - x_{k-1}) \le f*$$

$$- - - - - - - - - - - - - - - - - -$$

$$f(x_{k-m}) + (\partial f(x_{k-m}), x - x_{k-m}) \le f*$$

(8)

and its solution is taken as x_{k+1}. The value $m \ge 0$ is arbitrary and may depend on k. In particular, with m = 0 the method is identical to the subgradient algorithm (2),(4) with $\lambda = 1$. If m is smaller, then instead of (8) it is more convenient to solve the dual problem

$$\min \{ \frac{1}{2} \| \sum_{i=k-m}^{k} \lambda_i \partial f(x_i) \|^2 - \sum_{i=k-m}^{k} \lambda_i (f(x_i) - f* - (\partial f(x_i), x_i - x_k)):$$

$$\lambda_i \ge 0 \}$$

(9)

and, denoting its solution as λ_i^k, to obtain

$$x_{k+1} = x_k - \sum_{i=k-m}^{k} \lambda_i^k \, \partial f(x_i) \quad . \tag{10}$$

This form of stating the method shows that it is quite closely related to the steepest descent, the conjugate subgradient, and other methods. Reference [10] shows that the method (8) converges at least no more slowly than the subgradient method (2),(4) with $\lambda = 1$. Moreover, if $f(x)$ is a piecewise-linear function with a non-singular minimum and $m \geq N$, the method is finite. The latter property is a great advantage of the method, although, firstly, one needs to know f^* and, secondly, for large m the auxiliary problem 8) or (9,10) is rather laborious.

1 a number of his works [21,22,23,24,25,26] N.Z. Shor has suggested that space metric be transformed at each iteration to accelerate convergence of the subgradient method. A general algorithm for such an approach is in the following: let $s \in R^n$, $\| s \| = 1$, $\alpha \geq 0$. Then a linear operator $R_\alpha(s)$ such that

$$R_\alpha(s)x = x + (\alpha - 1)ss^t x \tag{11}$$

is referred to as the space-dilation operator acting in the direction s with a coefficient α. It is clear that $R_\alpha(s)s = \alpha s$, and for x orthogonal to s, $R_\alpha(s)x = x$. By making the transformations of the space $R_{\alpha_k}(s_k)$ at each step, computing subgradients for the new variables, and then transforming back to the original variables, we shall have the method

$$x_{k+1} = x_k - \gamma_k P_k P_k^t \partial f(x_k) \quad ,$$

$$P_k = P_{k-1} R_{\alpha_k^{-1}}(s_k) \quad , \qquad P_0 = I \quad . \tag{12}$$

N.Z. Shor has considered two feasible versions for selecting directions s_k. The first [21,22,24,25] provides dilation of the space in the direction of a subsequent subgradient, i.e.

$s_k = \partial f(x_k)$. Let us put down this method in a symmetrical form suggested by V.A. Skokov [27]:

$$x_{k+1} = x_k + \gamma_k p_k \quad , \quad p_k = -H_k \partial f(x_k) \quad ,$$

$$H_k = H_{k-1} + \left(1 - \frac{1}{\alpha_k^2}\right)\frac{p_{k-1} p_{k-1}^t}{(\partial f(x_{k-1}), p_{k-1})} \quad , \quad H_0 = I \quad . \tag{13}$$

Obviously, the matrices H_k are symmetric. In the above papers a number of ways to select the parameters γ_k and α_k are considered. In particular if f* and the constant M > 1 are known in the inequality

$$(\partial f(x), x - x^*) \le M(f(x) - f^*) \quad , \tag{14}$$

one may choose

$$\gamma_k = \left(\frac{2M}{M + 1}\right)\left(\frac{f(x_k) - f^*}{\| \partial f(x_k) \|^2}\right) \quad ,$$

$$\alpha_k = \alpha = \frac{M + 1}{M - 1} \tag{15}$$

Theorem 5 [22]

Let f(x) be convex and continuous and let the condition (14) hold. Then the algorithm (13),(15) converges geometrically with the rate $\alpha^{-1/N}$:

$$\lim \inf \alpha^{k/N}(f(x_k) - f^*) < \infty \quad .$$

A result for the extreme case $\alpha_k = \infty$ and

$$\gamma_k = \frac{2(f(x_k) - f^*)}{\| p_k \|^2} \tag{16}$$

is also known.

Theorem 6 [22,27]

If $f(x)$ is quadratic, then in the method (13),(16) $x_N = x^*$, and $H_N = 0$. In other words, for a quadratic case the method (16) is finite and coincides with one of the known orthogonalization methods for solving systems of linear equations.

The second version of the method [23,24,25,26] provides space dilation in the direction of the difference of two sequential subgradients, i.e. $s_k = \partial f(x_k) - \partial f(x_{k-1})$. In the statement of [27] the method takes the form

$$x_{k+1} = x_k + \gamma_k p_k \quad , \quad p_k = -H_k \partial f(x_k) \quad ,$$

$$e_k = \partial f(x_k) - \partial f(x_{k-1}) \quad , \tag{17}$$

$$H_k = H_{k-1} - (1 - \frac{1}{\alpha_k^2})\frac{H_{k-1}e_k e_k^t H_{k-1}}{(H_{k-1}e_k, e_k)} \quad , \quad H_0 = I \quad .$$

Unlike all other versions of the subgradient method, the step size is chosen from the condition of the steepest descent:

$$\gamma_k = \arg \min_{\gamma} f(x_k + \gamma p_k) \quad . \tag{18}$$

In practical computations the value α_k was taken equal to 2 or 3 and further increase of α_k did not affect the convergence rate. References [23,24,25,26] describe certain conditions that guarantee the convergence of the algorithm. Its rate of convergence has not been given enough attention.

Consider an extreme version of the method, $\alpha_k = \infty$.

Theorem 7 [26,27]

Let $\alpha_k = \infty$ and $f(x)$ be quadratic. Then in the method (17),18)

$$x_N = x^* \quad , \quad H_N = 0 \quad .$$

The method (17),(18) in this case is reduced to one of the versions of the conjugate directions method [28].

Thus, the subgradient methods with space dilation are conceptually close to variable-metric methods used for minimization of smooth functions, and their limiting versions have the property that they are finite for quadratic functions. The important question of the convergence rate for space-dilation methods for essentially nonsmooth functions (e.g. piecewise-linear) remains unanswered.

3. EXTENSIONS

We have thus far discussed unconditional minimization of a convex continuous function on R^N. Now let us concentrate on the potential of the subgradient method in solving more general problems.

(a) *Infinite-Dimensional Space*. Let it be required to find the minimum of the convex continuous functional f(x) in the Hilbert space H. The subgradient $\partial f(x)$ is in this case defined exactly as in (1) and the subgradient method has the same form as (2). It has been proved [6] that the theorem on convergence of the method (2),(3) remains valid even in Hilbert spaces, and the same has been proved [10] for the methods (2),(4), and (8). Nevertheless some of the methods of Section 2 (e.g. the center-of-gravity method) are specific to finite-dimensional spaces.

(b) *Problems with Constraints*. Let us consider the minimization problem with constraints

$$\min f(x) \quad , \quad x \in H$$

$$g(x) \leq 0 \tag{19}$$

$$x \in Q \quad ,$$

where f and g are continuous convex functionals and Q is a convex closed set. An arbitrary problem of convex programming can be reduced to the form (19). Thus if there are several constraints

$g_i(x) \leq 0$, $i = 1,\ldots m$ then it can be assumed that

$$g(x) = \max_i g_i(x)$$

or

$$g(x) = \sum_{i=1}^m g_i(x)_+ \quad .$$

The set Q is assumed to be of simple structure; in particular, the problem of finding a projection onto Q has a simple solution. The cases of

$$Q = \{x \in R^N : a \leq x \leq b\} \quad , \quad Q = \{x \in H : \|x - a\| \leq r\}$$

are typical. Reference [6] has proposed an extension of the sub-gradient method for solution of (19):

$$x_{k+1} = P_Q(x_k - \gamma_k s_k)$$

$$s_k = \begin{cases} \partial f(x_k)/\| \partial f(x_k) \| & \text{if} \quad g(x_k) \leq 0 \qquad (20) \\ \partial g(x_k)/\| \partial g(x_k) \| & \text{if} \quad g(x_k) > 0 \quad , \end{cases}$$

where P_Q is the projection operator on Q and convergence of this method has been proved under the condition (3).

(c) *Nonconvex Functions.* The function $f(x)$ to be minimized has thus far been assumed convex. Now let us consider the case of quasiconvex functions (such that the sets $\{x : f(x) \leq C\}$ are convex). In this case the subgradient at the point x_k can be re-placed by a vector s_k which is support for the set $\{x : f(x) \leq f(x_k)\}$, i.e. $(s_k, x - x_k) \leq 0$ for all x such that $f(x) \leq f(x_k)$. It can be proved [6] that with this replacement the method retains conver-gence under the assumptions made in the convex case.

Another generalization of greater importance is using nearly-differentiable functions [25]. A generalized gradient of f at x is a vector $s = \lim\limits_{k\to\infty} \nabla f(x_k)$, where $x_k \to x$ is an arbitrary sequence of points where the gradient exists. For convex continuous $f(x)$ the set of generalized gradients coincides with the set of subgradients. References [25,29] have proved the convergence of the method (2) where the subgradient is replaced by the generalized gradient. A somewhat different important class of weakly convex functions to which the subgradient method can be extended has been studied by E.A. Nurminskii [30,31].

(d) *Non-Unique Minimum.* Let the set X^* of the minimum points of minima of the convex continuous function $f(x)$ on the convex closed set Q consist of more than one point. Then the subgradient minimization method is nonstable, in the sense that for different initial points it can converge to different solutions (and for some variants of the method even that cannot be guaranteed). In a similar way, in the infinite-dimensional case the subgradient method may not converge even if there is a unique minimum solution. This kind of problem can be solved by using a regularization method. A regularizing function $f_1(x)$ is chosen that is strictly convex (in the infinite-dimensional case uniformly convex), e.g. $f_1(x) = \| x \|^2$. There is a unique point x_k minimizing the regularized function $f(x) + \alpha_k f_1(x)$, where $\alpha_k > 0$ is the regularization parameter. Then it can be shown [32] that $x_k \to x^*$ as $\alpha_k \to 0$ where x^* is the point in the set of minimum points of $f(x)$ on Q for which $f_1(x)$ is minimal. The subgradient method can then be made stable by using this idea. Consider the method

$$x_{k+1} = P_Q[x_k - \gamma_k(\partial f(x_k) + \alpha_k \partial f_1(x_k))] \quad . \tag{21}$$

In other words, one step of the subgradient method for minimization of the regularized function is made; following this, the regularization parameter is changed.

Theorem 8 [33]

Let $f(x)$ and $f_1(x)$ be convex continuous functions on R^N, let $f_1(x)$ be strongly convex, let Q be a convex closed and bounded set, and let $\alpha_k \to 0, \gamma_k/\alpha_k \to 0, \sum \gamma_k \alpha_k = \infty, \alpha_k/\alpha_{k+1} = 1 + 0(\gamma_k \alpha_k)$ (for in-stance $\gamma_k = k^{-1/2}$, $\alpha_k = k^{-\rho}$, $0 < \rho < 1/2$). Then in the method (21) $x_k \to x^*$, where $x^* = \arg\min_{x \in X^*} f_1(x)$, $X^* = \text{Arg}\min_{x \in Q} f(x)$.

(e) *A Continuous Analog of the Subgradient Method.* To the discrete gradient method, $x_{k+1} = x_k - \gamma_k \nabla f(x_k)$, there corresponds the continuous analog $\dot{x} = -\nabla f(x)$. Similarly there exists a continuous version of the subgradient method

$$\dot{x} \in -\partial f(x) \quad . \tag{22}$$

Methods of this type have been in use (without much justification) since the mid-fifties for solution of linear programming problems on analog computers. To prove that (22) converges is a non-trivial matter, however, since (22) is a differential equation with a mul-tivalued discontinuous right-hand side; therefore its solution needs an appropriate definition. The existence of a solution to such an equation also needs special study. References [34,35,36] deal with this subject.

(f) *The Subgradient Method for Finding Saddle Points.* The point

$$x^* \in Q \subset R^n, y^* \in S \subset R^m$$

is called a saddle point of the function $\phi(x,y)$ on $Q \times S$ if

$$\phi(x,y^*) \geq \phi(x^*,y^*) \geq \phi(x^*,y)$$

for all

$$x \in Q, \ y \in S$$

or

$$\min_{x \in Q} \max_{y \in S} \phi(x,y) = \phi(x^*,y^*) = \max_{y \in S} \min_{x \in Q} \phi(x,y) \quad .$$

If the function $\phi(x,y)$ is smooth, then to minimize it the gradient method can be applied:

$$x_{k+1} = P_Q(x_k - \gamma_k \nabla_x \phi(x_k,y_k)) \quad ,$$

$$y_{k+1} = P_S(y_k + \gamma_k \nabla_y \phi(x_k,y_k)) \quad .$$

The similar subgradient algorithm for a nonsmooth case has been proposed in [5,37]:

$$x_{k+1} = P_Q(x_k - \gamma_k \partial_x \phi(x_k,y_k))$$

$$y_{k+1} = P_S(y_k + \gamma_k \partial_y \phi(x_k,y_k)) \quad .$$

(23)

The method (23) has been validated in [38]. The function $\phi(x,y)$ is called stable [38] if for all $x^* \in X^*$, $y^* \in Y^*$ ($X^* \times Y^*$ is the set of saddle points of $\phi(x,y)$ on $Q \times S$) one has

$$\text{Arg} \min_{x \in Q} \phi(x,y^*) = X^* \quad , \quad \text{Arg} \max_{y \in S} \phi(x^*,y) = Y^* \quad .$$

In particular, if $\phi(x,y)$ is strictly convex with respect to x and strictly concave with respect to y, then it is stable.

Theorem 9 [38]

Let $\phi(x,y)$ be continuous on $R^n \times R^m$, convex with respect to x for all $y \in S$, concave with respect to y for all $x \in Q$, and stable, let the sets Q and S be convex, closed and bounded, and let $\gamma_k \to 0$, $\sum \gamma_k = \infty$. Then in the method (23),

$$\rho(x_k, X^*) \to 0 \quad , \quad \rho(y_k, Y^*) \to 0 \quad .$$

Results on the convergence of (23) in infinite-dimensional spaces have been given in [33].

The convergence of the method (23) without stability (e.g. for the Lagrange function in a convex programming problem) remains an open question. For the smooth case and with stability only with respect to x, this question has been answered in [39]. In the general case the method can be modified by regularization [33].

$$x_{k+1} = P_Q[x_k - \gamma_k(\partial_x\phi(x_k,y_k) + \alpha_k\partial f_1(x_k))]$$

$$y_{k+1} = P_S[y_k + \gamma_k(\partial_y\phi(x_k,y_k) - \alpha_k\partial f_2(y_k))] \quad , \tag{24}$$

where $f_1(x), f_2(y)$ are strongly convex functions.

In [33] convergence of this method has been proved under the same assumptions on γ_k, α_k as in Theorem 8. No strict convexity-concavity or stability of $\phi(x,y)$ is needed.

(g) *Difference Approximation of the Subgradient.* In a number of problems the subgradients $\partial f(x)$ are inaccessible and only values $f(x)$ at arbitrary points are known. In this case the subgradient $\partial f(x)$ can probably be replaced by its finite-difference approximation, e.g. by the vector

$$s(x,\alpha) = \sum_{i=1}^{N} \frac{f(x + \alpha e_i) - f(x - \alpha e_i)}{2\alpha} e_i \quad , \tag{25}$$

where e_i are coordinate orths; α is the size of the test step. This procedure works, however, only in the smooth case; it may stop at non-minimum points when minimizing a nondifferentiable convex function. Convergence may be obtained by introducing additional smoothing through randomization. One of the simplest methods of this type was proposed by A.M. Gupal [40]:

$$x_{k+1} = x_k - \gamma_k s(y_k,\alpha_k)$$

$$y_k = x_k + \alpha_k z_k \quad , \tag{26}$$

where Z_k is a random vector uniformly distributed on a unit sphere and $s(y,\alpha)$ is computed by formula (25). It has been proved [4] that with a certain ratio of the step sizes α_k, γ_k (namely, with $\sum \gamma_k = \infty$, $\sum \gamma_k^2 < \infty$, $\alpha_k \to 0$, $\gamma_k/\alpha_k \to 0$, $\frac{\alpha_k - \alpha_{k+1}}{\alpha_k \gamma_k} \to 0$) and under some natural assumptions on $f(x)$, this method does converge. In [41] a similar method was used for minimization of discontinuous as well as nondifferentiable functions.

4. THE SUBGRADIENT METHOD IN THE PRESENCE OF NOISE

In many real-world problems the gradient or the subgradient cannot be precisely computed (for instance in system parameter estimation, identification, learning, and pattern recognition [42,43]) because of incomplete data on the function to be minimized which is the expected value of a certain quantity whose distribution law is not exactly known. In other cases the errors are caused by computation errors, experimentation in a real process, etc. In any case, usually we know only an approximate value of the vector $\partial f(x)$, denoted as $\partial F(x)$. The error

$$\xi(x) = \partial F(x) - \partial f(x) \tag{27}$$

may contain both the random and the deterministic components $\eta(x)$ and $a(x)$:

$$M\xi(x) = a(x) \quad , \quad \eta(x) = \xi(x) - a(x) \quad , \quad M\eta(x) = 0 \quad . \tag{28}$$

Then the subgradient method for minimizing $f(x)$ on R^N is of the form

$$x_{k+1} = x_k - \gamma_k \partial F(x_k) \quad . \tag{29}$$

The pioneering effort in the study of stochastic methods of the form (29) was made by Yu.M. Ermol'ev [44,45,46]. His investigations and those of his followers have been summarized in a monograph [47] and a survey [48]. Among other works on optimization methods in the presence of random noise, the book by V.Ya. Katkovnik [49] is worth mentioning. The methods of type (29) may be regarded as Robbins-Monro stochastic approximation procedures, and the results obtained in the theory of stochastic approximation (e.g. [43,47,50,51]) can be used in their analysis.

Let us cite a simple result on convergence of the algorithm (29). Its modifications and extensions (deterministic errors, nonunique or nonexistent extremum, noise with infinite variance, mean square convergence, etc.) are to be found in [46,47,52,53, 54].

Theorem 10

Let $f(x)$ be convex, and continuous and have a unique minimum point $x^* \in R^N$; suppose the noise $\xi(x)$ is purely random, is independent at different points, and has a mean $M\xi(x) = 0$, and a variance $\sigma^2(x) = M\|\xi(x)\|^2$, and assume the following constraints on the growth of $\partial f(x)$ and $\sigma^2(x)$:

$$\|\partial f(x)\|^2 \leq C_1(1 + \|x - x^*\|^2) \quad,$$

$$\sigma^2(x) \leq C_2(1 + \|x - x^*\|^2) \quad,$$

(30)

Let γ_k satisfy the condition

$$\sum_{k=0}^{\infty} \gamma_k = \infty \quad, \quad \sum_{k=0}^{\infty} \gamma_k^2 < \infty \quad.$$

(31)

Then in the method (29), $x_k \to x^*$ with a probability 1.

As for convergence rate, it can be shown [47,55] that if the condition $f(x) \geq f^* + \ell\|x - x^*\|^2$, $\ell > 0$ or $f(x) \geq f^* + \ell\|x - x^*\|$, $\ell > 0$ is valid, and given the choice $\gamma_k = \gamma/k$ ($\gamma > 0$ being large enough), then the rate of decrease of order $0(k^{-1})$ can be guaranteed for $\|x_k - x^*\|^2$ in some probabilistic sense. This is, generally speaking, the highest possible rate of convergence. Thus for

$$f(x) = x^2, x \in R^1, M\xi^2(x) = \sigma^2 > 0 \quad ,$$

the iterative process (29) with any method of selecting the step size cannot decrease the value of Mx_k^2 faster than $0(k^{-1})$ [56].

On the contrary, for the functions satisfying the condition (5), and with constrained noise

$$\| \xi(x) \| \leq c < \ell \tag{32}$$

and a step-size rule of type (6), there is geometric convergence.

Theorem 11 [57]

Let $f(x)$ be convex and continuous and the conditions (5) and (32) hold. Then for any x_0 there are γ_0 and $q < 1$ such that with $\gamma_k = \gamma_0 q^k$ the estimate $\| x_k - x^* \| \leq \| x_0 - x^* \| q^k$ is valid for the method (29).

The extensions of the subgradient method in Section 3 are, as a rule, applicable to problems in the presence of noise. Thus a stochastic analog of the method (20) has been proposed [58]. E.A. Nurminskii has applied the stochastic subgradient method to a class of non convex functions [59]. The iterative regularization method (21) in the presence of random noise has been discussed in Reference [60]. Finally, the behavior of the subgradient algorithm for finding saddle points (23) in the stochastic case has been studied in Reference [44,45,46,47] and in combination with the regularization method (an analog of (24)), in Reference [50].

REFERENCES

[1] Shor, N.Z., Generalized Gradient Methods for Non-Smooth
     Functions and Their Application to Mathematical Pro-
     gramming Problems, *EMM**, 12, 2 (1976), 332-356 (in
     Russian).

[2] Pshenichnyi, B.N., *Necessary Conditions for Extremum*,
     Nauka, Moscow, 1969 (English translation, Marcel
     Dekker, New York, 1971).

[3] Rockafellar, R.T., *Convex Analysis*, Princeton Univ. Press,
     Princeton, N.J., 1970.

[4] Shor, N.Z., *Application of the Gradient Method for the
     Solution of Network Transportation Problems*, Notes,
     Scientific Seminar on Theory and Application of Cyber-
     netics and Operations Research, Academy of Sciences,
     Kiev, 1962 (in Russian).

[5] Ermol'ev, Yu.M., Methods of Solution of Nonlinear Extremal
     Problems, *Kibern.**, 2, 4 (1966), 1-17; *Cybernetics*,
     2, 4, 1-16.

[6] Poljak, B.T., A General Method of Solving Extremal Problems,
     DAN*, 174, 1 (1967), 33-36; *Soviet Math. Doklady*, 8,
     593-597.

[7] Ermol'ev, Yu.M., and N.Z. Shor, On the Minimization of Non-
     Differentiable Functions, *Kibern.*, 3, 1 (1967), 101-
     102; *Cybernetics*, 3, 1, 72.

[8] Eremin, I.I., A Generalization of the Motzkin-Agmon Relaxa-
     tion Method, *Uspekhi Matematcheski Nauk*, 20, 2 (1965)
     (in Russian).

[9] Eremin, I.I., The Relaxation Method of Solving Systems of
     Inequalities with Convex Functions on the Left Sides,
     DAN, 160, 5 (1965), 994-996; *Soviet Math. Doklady*, 6,
     219-221.

[10] Poljak, B.T., Minimization of Unsmooth Functionals, *ZVMMF**,
     9, 3 (1969), 509-521; *USSR Computational Mathematics
     and Mathematical Physics*, 9, 14-29.

[11] Shor, N.Z., The Rate of Convergence of the Generalized
     Gradient Descent Method, *Kibern.*, 4, 3 (1968), 98-99;
     Cybernetics, 4, 3, 79-80.

*See list of abbreviations below.

[12] Shor, N.Z., and M.B. Schepakin, Algorithms for Solving Two-Stage Stochastic Programming Problems, *Kibern.*, 4, 3 (1968), 56-58; *Cybernetics*, 4, 3, 48-50.

[13] Shor, N.Z., and P.R. Gamburd, Certain Questions Concerning the Convergence of the Generalized Gradient Method, *Kibern.*, 7, 6 (1971), 82-84; *Cybernetics*, 7, 6, 1033-1036.

[14] Kelley, J.E., The Cutting-Plane Method for Solving Convex Programs, *Journal of the Society for Industrial and Applied Mathematics*, 8, 4 (1960), 703-712.

[15] Cheney, W., and A.A. Goldstein, Newton's Method for Convex Programming and Chebyshev Approximation, *Numerische Mathematik*, 1, 5 (1959), 253-268.

[16] Newman, D.J., Location of the Maximum on Unimodal Surfaces, *Journ. ACM*, 12, 3 (1965).

[17] Levin, A.Ju., On an Algorithm for the Minimization of Convex Functions, *DAN*, 160, 6 (1965), 1244-1247; *Soviet Math. Doklady*, 6, 286-290.

[18] Judin, D.B., and A.S. Nemirovskii, Evaluation of Information Complexity for Mathematical Programming Problems, *EMM*, 12, 1 (1976), 128-142 (in Russian).

[19] Judin, D.B., and A.S. Nemirovskii, Information Complexity and Effective Methods for Solving Convex Extremum Problems, *EMM*, 12, 2 (1976), 357-369 (in Russian).

[20] Kuzovkin, A.I., and V.M. Tihomirov, On a Quantity of Observations for Finding a Minimum of a Convex Function, *EMM*, 3, 1 (1967), 95-103 (in Russian).

[21] Shor, N.Z., Utilization of the Operation of Space Dilation in the Minimization of Convex Functions, *Kibern.*, 6, 1 (1970), 6-12, *Cybernetics*, 6, 1, 7-15.

[22] Shor, N.Z., Convergence Rate of the Gradient Descent Method with Dilation of Space, *Kibern.*, 6, 2 (1970), 80-85; *Cybernetics*, 6, 2, 102-108.

[23] Shor, N.Z., and N.G. Zhurbenko, A Minimization Method Using Space Dilation in the Direction of Difference of Two Successive Gradients, *Kibern.*, 7, 3 (1971), 51-59; *Cybernetics*, 7, 3, 450-459.

[24] Shor, N.Z., and L.P. Shabashova, Solution of Minimax Problems by the Generalized Gradient Method with Space Dilation, *Kibern.*, 8, 1 (1972), 82-88; *Cybernetics*, 8, 1, 88-94.

[25]   Shor, N.Z., A Class of Almost-Differentiable Functions and
       a Minimization Method for Functions of this Class,
       Kibern., 8, 4 (1972), 65-70; *Cybernetics*, 8, 4, 599-
       606.

[26]   Shor, N.Z., Convergence of a Gradient Method with Space
       Dilation in the Direction of the Difference Between
       Two Successive Gradients, *Kibern.*, 11, 4 (1975),
       48-53; *Cybernetics*, 11, 4, 564-570.

[27]   Shokov, V.A., Note on Minimization Methods Using Space
       Dilation, *Kibern.*, 10, 4 (1974), 115-117; *Cybernetics*,
       10, 4, 689-692.

[28]   Pshenichnyi, B.N., and Yu.M. Danilin, *Numerical Methods for
       Extremum Problems*, Nauka, Moscow, 1975 (in Russian).

[29]   Bazhenov, L.G., On the Convergence Conditions of the
       Minimization Method of Almost-Differentiable Functions,
       Kibern., 8, 4 (1972), 71-72; *Cybernetics*, 8, 4, 607-
       609.

[30]   Nurminskii, E.A., Convergence Conditions for Nonlinear
       Programming Algorithms, *Kibern.*, 8, 6 (1972), 79-81;
       Cybernetics, 8, 6, 959-962.

[31]   Nurminskii, E.A., The Quasigradient Method for Solving of
       the Nonlinear Programming Problems, *Kibern.*, 9, 1
       (1973), 122-125; *Cybernetics*, 9, 1, 145-150.

[32]   Levitin, E.S., and B.T. Poljak, Convergence of Minimizing
       Sequences in Conditional Extremum Problems, *DAN*, 168,
       5 (1966), 993-996; *Soviet Math. Doklady*, 7 (1966),
       764-767.

[33]   Bakushinskii, A.B., and B.T. Poljak, On the Solution of
       Variational Inequalities, *DAN*, 219, 5 (1974), 1038-
       1041; *Soviet Math. Doklady*, 15 (1974), 1705-1710.

[34]   Karpinskaja, N.N., Methods of Penalty Functions and Founda-
       tions of Pyne's Method, *AT**, 28 (1967), 140-146;
       Automation and Remote Control, 28, 124-129.

[35]   Kupatadze, O.V., On the Gradient Method for Unsmooth
       Functions Minimization, *Optimalnye i Adaptivnye
       Sistemy*, Trudy 4 Vsesojuzn. Sovesch. po Avt. Upr.
       (Tbilisi, 1968), Nauka, Moscow, 1972 (in Russian).

[36]   Korovin, S.K., and V.I. Utkin, Method of Piecewise Smooth
       Penalty Functions, *AT*, 37 (1976), 94-105; *Automation and
       Remote Control*, 37, 39-48.

---

*See list of abbreviations below.

[37] Mikhalevich, V.S., and Yu.M. Ermol'ev, V.V. Skurba, N.Z.
      Shor, Complex Systems and the Solution of Extremal
      Problems, *Kibern.*, 3, 5 (1967), 29-39; *Cybernetics*,
      3, 5, 25-34.

[38] Gol'stein, E.G., Generalized Gradient Method for Finding
      Saddle Points, *EMM*, 8, 4 (1970) (in Russian).

[39] Majstrovsky, G.D., On Gradient Method for Saddle Points
      Searching, *EMM*, 12, 5 (1976), 917-929 (in Russian).

[40] Gupal, A.M., On a Minimization Method for Almost-Differ-
      entiable Functions, *Kibern.*, 13, 1 (1977), 114-116.

[41] Gupal, A.M., and V.I. Norkin, A Minimization Algorithm
      for Discontinuous Functions, *Kibern.*, 13, 2 (1977),
      73-75.

[42] Tsypkin, Ja.Z., *Adaptation and Learning in Automatic
      Systems*, Nauka, Moscow, 1968 (English translation,
      Academic Press, New York, 1971).

[43] Aizerman, M.A., E.M. Braverman, and L.I. Rozonoer, *Poten-
      tial Functions Method in Machine Learning Theory*,
      Nauka, Moscow, 1970 (in Russian).

[44] Ermol'ev, Yu.M., and V.V. Nekrylova, Some Methods of
      Stochastic Optimization, *Kibern.*, 2, 6 (1966), 96-98;
      Cybernetics, 9, 4, 691-693.

[45] Ermol'ev, Yu.M., and N.Z. Shor, The Method of Random Walk
      for the Two-Stage Problem of Stochastic Programming
      and its Generalizations, *Kibern.*, 4, 1 (1968), 90-92;
      Cybernetics, 4, 1, 59-60.

[46] Ermol'ev, Yu.M., On the Method of Generalized Stochastic
      Gradients and Stochastic Quasi-Fejer Sequences,
      Kibern., 5, 2 (1969), 73-84; *Cybernetics*, 5, 2, 208-
      220.

[47] Ermol'ev, Yu.M., *Stochastic Programming Methods*, Nauka,
      Moscow, 1976 (in Russian).

[48] Ermol'ev, Yu.M., Stochastic Models and Methods of Optimiza-
      tion, *Kibern.*, 11, 4 (1975), 109-119; *Cybernetics*,
      11, 4, 630-641.

[49] Katkovnik, V.Ja., *Linear Estimates and Stochastic Optimiza-
      tion Problems*, Nauka, Moscow, 1976 (in Russian).

[50] Nevel'son, M.B., and R.Z. Hasminskii, *Stochastic Approxima-
      tion and Recurrent Estimation*, Nauka, Moscow, 1972
      (in Russian).

[51] Poljak, B.T., Convergence and Convergence Rate of Iterative Stochastic Algorithms, I. General Case, *AT*, 37, 12 (1976), 83-94; *Automation and Remote Control*, 37, 1858-1868.

[52] Litvakov, B.M., Convergence of Recurrent Algorithms for Pattern Recognition Learning, *AT*, 29, (1968), 142-150; *Automation and Remote Control*, 29, 121-128.

[53] Litvakov, B.M., On a Class of Robbins-Monro Procedures, *Information Science*, 6, 1 (1973).

[54] Poljak, B.T., and Ja.Z. Tsypkin, Pseudogradient Adaptation and Learning, *AT*, 34, 6 (1973), 45-68; *Automation and Remote Control*, 34, 377-397.

[55] Guseva, O.V., Convergence Rate of the Method of Generalized Stochastic Gradients, *Kibern.*, 7, 4 (1971), 143-145; *Cybernetics*, 7, 4, 738-742.

[56] Tsypkin, Ja.Z., and B.T. Poljak, Attainable Accuracy of Adaptation Algorithms, *DAN*, 218, 3 (1974), 532-535.

[57] Poljak, B.T., Nonlinear Programming Methods in the Presence of Noise, in *Proceedings of the 9th International Symposium on Mathematical Programming*, Budapest, 1976, North-Holland, Amsterdam, 1977.

[58] Gupal, A.M., One Stochastic Programming Problem with Constraint of a Probabilistic Nature, *Kibern.*, 10, 6 (1974), 94-100; *Cybernetics*, 10, 6, 1019-1026.

[59] Nurminskii, E.A., Convergence Conditions of Stochastic Programming Algorithms, *Kibern.*, 9, 3 (1973), 84-87; *Cybernetics*, 9, 3, 464-468.

[60] Poljak, B.T., Stochastic Regularized Algorithms, in *Suppl. to Preprints, Stochastic Control Symp. IFAC*, Budapest, Sept. 25-27, 1974.

Abbreviations of Russian Journal Titles

EMM   - Ekonomika i Matematicheskie Metody (Economics and
           Mathematical Methods)

*Kibern. - Kibernetika (Kiev)

*DAN   - Doklady Academii Nauk SSSR (Soviet Mathe. Doklady)

*ZVMMF   - Zurnal Vycislitel'noi Mathematiki i Matematiceskoi
           Fiziki (Journal of Computational Mathematics and
           Mathematical Physics)

*AT   - Avtomatika i Telemehanika (Automation and Remote
           Control)

---

*These journals are translated into English.

NONDIFFERENTIABLE OPTIMIZATION AND THE RELAXATION METHOD*

J. L. Goffin

1. INTRODUCTION

The relaxation method for solving systems of linear inequalities, as defined by Agmon [1] and Motzkin and Schoenberg [7], is closely connected to the relaxation method for solving systems of linear equalities. The relationship was made precise in Agmon's paper.

Subgradient optimization is a technique that attempts to solve the problem of maximizing a general, maybe nondifferentiable, concave function (or minimizing a convex function). One of the main expectations from subgradient optimization is that it could be used to solve some large-scale problems; computational results reported in [5] and [6] gave some credence to that idea. Subgradient optimization is closely related to the relaxation method for solving systems of linear inequalities, which has been used with success on some very large-scale problems with special structure: this seems to justify a closer look at subgradient optimization.

In this paper we will make explicit the relationship between the relaxation method for linear inequalities and subgradient optimization. The speed of convergence of both methods depends on condition numbers which have been defined in [3] and [4]. It will be shown that the two theorems on convergence are almost identical.

*This research was supported in part by the D.G.E.S. (Quebec) and the N.R.C. of Canada under grant A4152.

2.   THE RELAXATION METHOD AND SUBGRADIENT OPTIMIZATION

Let $<\alpha^i,x> + \beta^i \geq 0$, $i \in I$ be a finite system of linear inequalities where $\alpha^i \in R^n$, $\beta^i \in R$, $x \in R^n$. (2.1)

Let $P = \{x \in R^n: \ <\alpha^i,x> + \beta^i \geq 0, \ \forall \ i \in I\}$, the solution set.

Define the function f_1 by:

$$f_1(x) = Min \ \{<\alpha^i,x> + \beta^i, i \in I\}$$

and let f_1^* be the maximum of $f(x)$.   It is clear that

$$f_1^* > 0 \ => \ dim \ P = n \quad ;$$

$$f_1^* < 0 \ => \ P \ is \ empty \quad .$$

If we define $f(x) = Min \ \{0,f_1(x)\}$, it follows that P is not empty if and only if $\underset{x \in R^n}{Max} \ f(x) = 0$, and that P is the set of points on which f assumes its maximum value.   Furthermore, P is empty if and only if $\underset{x \in R^n}{Max} \ f(x) = \underset{x \in R^n}{Max} \ f_1(x) = f_1^* < 0$; the set of points on which f assumes its maximum value has been defined as the Chebyshev solution to the infeasible system of linear inequalities.

If we let $a^i = \dfrac{\alpha^i}{\| \alpha^i \|}$, $b^i = \dfrac{\beta^i}{\| \alpha^i \|}$ (we assume that $\alpha_i \neq 0$ $\forall i \in I$), where $\| \ \|$ means the Euclidean norm, then the system

$$<a^i,x> + b^i \geq 0 \quad , \quad\quad\quad i \in I \quad\quad\quad\quad (2.2)$$

is equivalent to (2.1).

Let $w_1(x) = Min \ \{<a^i,x> + b^i, i \in I\}$ and $w(x) = Min \ \{w_1(x),0\}$; also let $w^* = \underset{x}{Max} \ w(x)$.

Clearly $\{x \in R^n: w(x) = w^*\} = P$ provided that P is not empty (and $w^* = 0$).   If P is empty then $w^* < 0$, and the set of x which maximizes $w(x)$ is not necessarily the same as the set of x which maximizes f(x) (it is clear though that f* < 0 iff w* < 0). The functions f, f_1, w, w_1 are all concave and piecewise-linear.

A "subgradient" set can be defined for each x and each concave function, say w_1:

$$\partial w_1(x) = \{v \in R^n : \ w_1(y) \leq w_1(x) + <v, y - x>, \ y \in R^n\} \ .$$

Letting $Iw_1(x) = \{i \in I: \ w_1(x) = <a^i, x> + b^i\}$, then $\partial w_1(x) = Conv\{a^i : i \in Iw_1(x)\}$, where Conv means convex hull. Let $I_w(x) = \{i \in I: \ w(x) = <a^i, x> + b^i\}$. It can be seen that

$$\partial w(x) = \partial w_1(x) \qquad\qquad \text{if } x \not\in P$$

$$\partial w(x) = Conv(\partial w_1(x) \cup \{0\}) \qquad \text{if } x \in bd \ P$$

$$\partial w(x) = \{0\} \qquad\qquad \text{if } x \in int \ P$$

(where bd P means boundary of P and int P means the interior of P).

The same definitions and ideas are of course valid for f and f_1.

Three different implementations of the relaxation method have been given by Agmon--the maximal distance, the maximal residual, and the cyclical methods.

Let

$$H^i = \{x: \ <\alpha^i, x> + \beta^i \geq 0\} = \{x: \ <a^i, x> + b^i \geq 0\}$$

and

$$E^i = \{x: \ <\alpha^i, x> + \beta^i = 0\} = \{x: \ <a^i, x> + b^i = 0\} \ .$$

The notation d(x,S) will indicate the distance between a point x and a set S. Clearly,

$$d(x,E^i) = \frac{|<\alpha^i,x> + \beta^i|}{||\alpha^i||} = |<a^i,x> + b^i|$$

$$d(x,H^i) = \frac{\text{Max} \ (-(<\alpha^i,x> + \beta^i),0)}{||\alpha^i||} = \text{Max} \ (-(<a^i,x> + b^i),0) \quad .$$

Note that $w(x) = - \underset{i \in I}{\text{Max}} \ d(x,H^i)$.

The relaxation method applied to (2.1) constructs a sequence of points in the following manner.

2.2.1 Choose $x^o \in R^n$ arbitrary.

2.2.2 If $x^q \in P$, the sequence terminates.
If $x^q \notin P$, then determine i^q by one of the three methods below.

    2.2.2.1 The maximal distance method:
        let i^q be the index of a halfspace H^i which is
        the furthest distance away from x^q; i.e.,
        $d(x^q,H^{i^q}) \geq d(x^q,H^i) \ \forall i \in I.$

    2.2.2.2 The maximal residual method:
        let i^q be the index of a most violated constraint;
        i.e., $<\alpha^{i^q},x^q> + \beta^{i^q} \leq <\alpha^i,x^q> + \beta^i \ \forall i \in I.$

    2.2.2.3 The cyclical method:
        assume that $I = \{1,2,3,\ldots,m\}$, then take
        $i^q = q + 1 \,(\text{mod } m).$

2.2.3 Then set

$$x^{q+1} = x^q + \sigma_q \ d(x^q,H^{i^q}) \ \frac{\alpha^{i^q}}{||\alpha^{i^q}||} \quad ,$$

where usually $\sigma_q \in (0,2]$, and go back to 2.2.2 with $q \leftarrow q + 1.$

In the cyclical method it is quite possible that $d(x^q, H^{i^q}) = 0$, so that no move is taken at Step 3. We will not discuss it, as it does not seem easy to compare it to subgradient optimization.

If $\sigma_q = 1$ then x^{q+1} is the orthogonal projection of x^q on H^{i^q}; if $\sigma_q = 2$, then x^{q+1} is the reflexion of x^q on E^{i^q}; if $\sigma_q \in (1,2)$ one talks of overprojection, and if $\sigma_q \in (0,1)$ of underprojection.

Now let us describe the subgradient optimization algorithm, say for the function f:

2.3.1 Choose $x^o \in R^n$.

2.3.2 Compute a subgradient of f at x^q: $u^q \in \partial f(x^q)$.
       If $u^q = 0$, an optimal point has been found.

2.3.3 The next point x^{q+1} of the sequence will be obtained
       by moving from x^q in the direction of u^q by a certain
       step size. Go back to 2.3.2 with q+1 replacing q.
       Various proposals have been made for the step size:

   2.3.3.1 Shor [10]: $x^{q+1} = x^q + \lambda_q \dfrac{u^q}{\| u^q \|}$ where $\lambda_q > 0$.

   2.3.3.2 Held and Karp [5]: $x^{q+1} = x^q + \rho_q u^q$ where
            $\rho_q > 0$.

   2.3.3.3 Held, Wolfe and Crowder [6], Eremin [2], Poljak
            [9], Oettli [8]:

$$x^{q+1} = x^q + \sigma_q \frac{\hat{f} - f(x^q)}{\| u^q \|^2} u^q \quad,$$

            where $\sigma_q > 0$ and $\hat{f} > f(x^q)$ is a guess of the
            optimal value f* of f(x) which can either be:

   2.3.3.3.1 an overestimate: $\hat{f} > f*$,

2.3.3.3.2 an underestimate: $\hat{f} < f*$,

2.3.3.3.3 the exact estimate: $\hat{f} = f*$.

It can now be seen that:

(i) The maximal distance relaxation method for solving
(2.1) (which is the same as the maximal residual
relaxation method for solving (2.2)) is equivalent to
the subgradient algorithm applied to the function
$w(x)$, using the step size given in 2.3.3.3.3 if P is
not empty, and the step size of 2.3.3.3.1 with $\hat{f} = 0$
if P is empty.

(ii) The maximal residual relaxation method for solving
(2.1) is equivalent to the subgradient algorithm
applied to the function $f(x)$, with the same use of
step size as above.

For the maximal distance relaxation method (2.2.2.1) it is
clear that the index i^q selected maximizes $d(x^q, H^i)$, and thus
satisfies

$$- (<a^{i^q}, x^q>) - b^{i^q} = \frac{-<\alpha^{i^q}, x^q> - \beta^{i^q}}{\| \alpha^{i^q} \|} = d(x^q, H^{i^q})$$

$$= \underset{i \in I}{\text{Max}} \; d(x^q, H^i) = -w(x^q) \quad ;$$

thus

$$i^q \in Iw(x^q) \qquad \text{and} \qquad a^{i^q} \in \partial w(x^q) \quad .$$

The only minor difference is that in subgradient optimiza-
tion we are explicitly permitted the use of any $v^q \in \partial w(x^q)$. It
would require the following extension of the relaxation method:
if $Iw(x^q)$, the set of indices of the most distant halfspaces,
contains more than one element, then any direction $v^q = \underset{i \in Iw(x^q)}{\sum} (x^q)$

$\eta_i \alpha^i$ can be used, where

$$\sum_{i \in Iw(x^q)} \eta_i = 1 \quad , \quad \eta_i \geq 0 \ \forall i \in Iw(x^q) \quad ,$$

and the next iterate would be:

$$x^{q+1} = x^q + \sigma_q \ \frac{-\langle v^q, x^q \rangle - c^q}{\| v^q \|} \ \frac{v^q}{\| v^q \|} \quad ,$$

with $c^q = \sum_{i \in Iw(x^q)} \eta_i b^i$. Note that

$$\langle v^q, x^q \rangle + c^q = \sum_{i \in Iw(x^q)} \eta_i (\langle a^i, x^q \rangle + b^i) = w(x^q) \quad ,$$

and that we are simply projecting in the direction of the half-space $\{x: \ \langle v^q, x \rangle + c^q \geq 0\}$. Also $\| v^q \| \leq 1$.

In the next section, on condition numbers and convergence rates, this distinction will require some attention.

One key point to notice is that if the system of inequalities (2.1) is feasible then w* = 0, and thus the maximum value of w(x) is known; that is exactly the case 2.3.3.3.3 of the subgradient optimization technique. That the step sizes are identical is trivial to check.

The identity between the maximal residual relaxation method and subgradient optimization as applied to f can be shown in the same fashion. In this case, also, if (2.1) is feasible then the maximum value of f(x) is also known to be equal to zero.

Now if the system (2.1) has no solution, it is clear that f* < 0 is not known, then the search for a Chebyshev solution to (2.1) becomes exactly equivalent to the problem of maximizing f(x), which can be solved through subgradient optimization (in the case where the objective value is not known). One of the first examples of subgradient optimization can be found in some work by Eremin [2] on Chebyshev solutions of incompatible systems of linear inequalities (as can the first result on convergence that I have seen). This also means that the results on rates of convergence of subgradient optimization gathered by Shor and the author are valid for the Chebyshev problem.

The main difference between the relaxation method for solving feasible systems of inequalities and the subgradient method for maximizing a concave function is that in the first case the optimal value of the objective is known, while in the second it is not. This has some implications for the theories of convergence for the two methods: in the first case a rule for the step size ($\sigma_q \in (0,2]$) can be given so that for each q, $d(x^{q+1},P) \leq d(x^q,P)$; in the second case no step size rule can guarantee the monotonic decrease of anything. This also implies that a cyclical rule is not easy to use in subgradient optimization as it would not be clear if one should move or not in a direction a^i.

3. CONDITION NUMBERS AND RATES OF CONVERGENCE

Condition numbers have been defined and rates of convergence studied, for the relaxation method by Agmon [1] and the author [3], and for subgradient optimization by Shor [11] and the author [4]. As the two methods are quite similar, it is not surprising that the similarity will extend to the study of rates of convergence. In what follows, we will refer extensively to [3] and [4].

The study will be made for the comparison of the maximal distance method applied to (2.1) (or equivalently to (2.2)) and subgradient optimization applied to w(x). The function w(x) has the property that every extreme point of $\partial w(x)$ has norm one (except possibly for $x \in P$, where 0 is a subgradient).

We want to emphasize that not all of the results that follow can be extended to the comparison of f and (2.1).

3.1   The Relaxation Method

We will assume that P is not empty. For every $x^* \in$ bd P, let

$$N_P(x^*) = \{v \in R^n: \quad <v, y - x^*> \leq 0, \forall y \in P\} \quad ,$$

the normal cone to P at x^*. The normal cone can be written as:

$$N_P(x^*) = \{v \in R^n: \quad v = - \sum_{i \in Iw(x^*)} \eta_i a_i, \eta_i \geq 0\} \quad .$$

For any $x \in R^n/P = \{x \in R^n: \quad x \notin P\}$, let $x^*(x)$ be the closest point to x in P. Then $x^*(x)$ can be characterized by the fact that

$$x - x^*(x) \in N_P(x^*(x)) \quad .$$

Define, for every $x^* \in$ bd P [3],

$$\mu^*(x^*) = \underset{\substack{v \in N_P(x^*) \\ \|v\| = 1}}{\text{Inf}} \quad \underset{i \in Iw(x^*)}{\text{Max}} \quad \{-<a^i, v>\} \quad .$$

It can be shown that $\mu^*(x^*) > 0$, and that

$$\mu^* = \underset{x^* \in \text{bd } P}{\text{Inf}} \quad \mu^*(x^*) > 0 \quad .$$

The definition of the condition number μ^* is a sharpened version of a similar quantity defined by Agmon [1].

It can be shown [3] that (remember that $w^* = 0$):

$$\mu^* d(x, P) \leq -w(x) \leq d(x, P) \quad ,$$

where $d(x, P) = \| x - x^*(x) \|$, the distance between x and P. Both bounds can be shown to be tight, and thus μ^* could be defined by

$$\mu* = \underset{x \in R^n/P}{\text{Inf}} \frac{-w(x)}{d(x,P)} \quad .$$

Having defined $\mu*$, it is very easy to prove the geometric convergence of the relaxation method, as one can show that

$$d^2(x^{q+1},P) \leq d^2(x^q,P) - \sigma_q(2 - \sigma_q) \, w^2(x^q)$$

$$\leq d^2(x^q,P) \, [1 - \sigma_q(2 - \sigma_q)\mu*^2] \quad .$$

It follows that, provided that $\sigma_q \in [0,2]$, then $d(x^{q+1},P) \leq d(x^q,P)$, so monotonic decrease is guaranteed; and also that if $\sigma_q \in [\varepsilon, 2 - \varepsilon]$, then

$$d(x^{q+1},P) \leq d(x^q,P) \, \sqrt{1 - \varepsilon\mu*^2} \quad ,$$

so that geometric convergence occurs.

Two other concepts, which are also trying to measure the well conditioning of a problem, were introduced in [3].

For $x* \in$ bd P, let

$$C_P(x*) = \{u \in R^n: \quad <a^i,u> \geq 0, \, \forall i \in Iw(x*)\} \quad ,$$

the tangent cone to P at $x*$. Clearly $N_P(x*)$ is the polar cone to $C_P(x*)$. A polytope P will be called obtuse if every tangent cone is obtuse:

$$-N_P(x*) \subseteq C_P(x*) \qquad \forall x* \in \text{bd P} \quad .$$

For a cone C, let $\nu(C)$ be the sine of the half aperture angle of the largest spherical cone contained in C, and let

$$\nu = \underset{x* \in \text{bd P}}{\text{Inf}} \, \nu(C_P(x*)) \quad .$$

It is clear that $\nu > 0$ iff dim $P = n$, and that $\nu \geq \frac{\sqrt{2}}{2}$ implies that P is obtuse. It can also be shown that $\mu^* \geq \nu$ [3]. It can then be shown that the maximal distance relaxation method applied to (2.1) or (2.2), assuming that dim $P = n$, converges finitely if:

     (i) P is obtuse and $\sigma_q \in [1,2]$ for all q;

or

     (ii) $\sigma_q \in \left[\dfrac{2}{1 + 2\nu\sqrt{1 - \nu^2}} + \varepsilon, 2 \right]$, where $\varepsilon > 0$, for all q .

Thus, it has been proved that, if dim $P = n$, there is a range of values of σ_q which leads to finite convergence, and to geometric convergence (until termination) [3].

3.2 Subgradient Optimization

For the concave function $w(x)$, a condition number can be defined:

$$\mu(x) = \underset{u \in \partial w(x)}{\mathrm{Inf}} \frac{\langle u, x^*(x) - x \rangle}{\| u \| \cdot \| x^*(x) - x \|} \quad ,$$

and

$$\mu = \underset{x \in R^n/P}{\mathrm{Inf}} \mu(x) \quad .$$

Rates of convergence for subgradient optimization depend upon this quantity.

Theorem 3.1 [4]

Let $\{x^q\}$ be a sequence which satisfies $x^{q+1} = x^q + \lambda_o \rho^q \dfrac{u^q}{\| u^q \|}$, where $u^q \in \partial w(x^q)$, $\lambda_o > 0$, $\rho \in (0,1)$.

Let

$$C = \text{Max} \left\{ \frac{1}{\rho} , \frac{\mu - \sqrt{\mu^2 - (1 - \rho^2)}}{1 - \rho^2} \right\} , \quad D = \frac{\mu + \sqrt{\mu^2 - (1 - \rho^2)}}{1 - \rho^2}$$

and

$$z(\mu) = \begin{cases} \sqrt{1 - \mu^2} & \text{if } \mu \leq \frac{\sqrt{2}}{2} \\ \\ \frac{1}{2\mu} & \text{if } \mu > \frac{\sqrt{2}}{2} . \end{cases}$$

Then:

(i) $\rho \geq z(\mu)$ and $d(x^0) \in [\lambda_o C, \lambda_o D]$ implies that for all
q: $d(x^q) \leq d(x^0) \rho^q$;

(ii) $\rho \geq z(\mu)$ and $d(x^0) < \lambda_o C$ implies that for all
q: $d(x^q) \leq \lambda_o C \rho^q$;

(iii) $\rho < z(\mu)$ or $d(x^0) > \lambda_o D$ may lead to convergence of
$\{x^q\}$ to a non optimal point.

Theorem 3.2

The condition numbers μ and $\mu*$ are equal.

Proof

This theorem can be proved in many different ways. It will
be proved here in a way that gives new definitions of μ and $\mu*$,
and also does not assume any other result.

By definition

$$\mu(x) = \underset{u \in \partial w(x)}{\text{Inf}} \frac{\langle u, x*(x) - x \rangle}{\| u \| \cdot \| x*(x) - x \|} .$$

But $\langle u, x*(x) - x \rangle$ is positive for any $u \in \partial w(x)$, and

$$\frac{\langle u, x*(x) - x \rangle}{\| u \| \cdot \| x*(x) - x \|}$$

is a quasiconcave function of u on the domain $\{u: <u,x^*(x) - x> \geq 0\}$; it thus follows that the infimum is attained at some of the extreme points of $\partial w(x)$; i.e.

$$\mu(x) = \min_{i\in Iw(x)} \frac{<a^i,x^*(x) - x>}{\| x^*(x) - x\|} \qquad \text{as } \| a^i\| = 1 \quad .$$

If one uses the definition of concavity for w, one gets, as $w(x^*(x)) = 0$:

$$<a^i,x^*(x) - x> \geq -w(x) \geq <a^j,x^*(x) - x>$$

for any $i \in Iw(x)$, $j \in Iw(x^*(x))$.

Furthermore, if $w'(x;\delta)$ denotes the directional derivative at x in the direction δ, then

$$w'(x; x^*(x) - x) = \inf_{i\in Iw(x)} <a^i,x^*(x) - x>$$

$$w'(x^*; x - x^*(x)) = \inf_{j\in Iw(x^*)} <a^j,x - x^*(x)> \quad ,$$

and thus:

$$w'(x; x^*(x) - x) \geq -w(x) \geq -w'(x^*; x - x^*(x)) \quad .$$

Define for every x:

$$\delta(x) = \frac{x^*(x) - x}{\| x^*(x) - x\|} \quad ;$$

then one has

$$w'(x; \delta(x)) \geq \frac{-w(x)}{d(x,P)} \geq -w'(x^*; -\delta(x)) \quad .$$

It is also clear that

$$\mu(x) = w'(x; \delta(x)) \quad ,$$

so

$$\mu = \inf_{x \in R^n/P} w'(x; \delta(x)) \quad .$$

Also,

$$-w'(x^*; -\delta(x)) = \sup_{j \in Iw(x^*)} <a^j, \delta(x)> \geq \mu^*(x^*)$$

as

$$-\delta(x) \in N_P(x^*) \quad , \quad \text{and} \quad \| \delta(x) \| = 1 \quad .$$

And

$$\inf_{x \in x^* + N_P(x^*)} \{-w'(x^*; -\delta(x))\} = \mu^*(x^*) \quad ,$$

so that

$$\mu^* = \inf_{x^* \in bd\ P} \inf_{\substack{-\delta \in N_P(x^*) \\ \| \delta \| = 1}} (-w'(x^*; -\delta)) \quad .$$

From this, it is clear that $\mu \geq \mu^*$ (this could also be concluded from Theorem 3.1 in [4]). Now to show that $\mu = \mu^*$, the simplest way is to use v and x* such that

$$\mu^* = \max_{i \in Iw(x^*)} <a^i, v>$$

where

$$v \in - N_p(x^*) \quad \text{and} \quad \| v \| = 1 \ .$$

Now for any $\alpha \geq 0$, one has that

$$x^*(x^* - \alpha v) = x^* \ ,$$

i.e., the projection of $x^* - \alpha v$ on P is x^*. So

$$\mu^* = \underset{i \in Iw(x^*)}{\text{Max}} \ \langle a^i, \frac{x^* - x}{\alpha} \rangle$$

where $x = x^* - \alpha v$ and $\alpha = \| x^* - x \| = d(x,P)$. But,

$$\langle a^i, x^* - x \rangle = \langle a^i, x^* \rangle + b^i - \langle a^i, x \rangle - b^i$$

$$= -\langle a^i, x \rangle - b^i$$

$$\text{as } \langle a^i, x^* \rangle + b^i = 0 \quad \forall i \in Iw(x^*) \ ;$$

so

$$\mu^* = \underset{i \in Iw(x^*)}{\text{Max}} \ \frac{-\langle a^i, x \rangle - b^i}{d(x,P)} \ .$$

It is easy to check that there exists $\varepsilon > 0$ such that $Iw(x^* - \eta v) \subseteq Iw(x^*)$ for any $0 \leq \eta \leq \varepsilon$. Thus, if $z = x^* - \varepsilon v$,

$$\frac{-w(z)}{d(z,P)} = \underset{i \ Iw(z)}{\text{Max}} \ \frac{-\langle a^i, z \rangle - b^i}{d(z,P)} \leq \mu^* \leq \underset{i \in I}{\text{Max}} \ \frac{-\langle a^i, z \rangle - b^i}{d(z,P)}$$

$$= \frac{-w(z)}{d(z,P)} \ .$$

This, by the way, proves that

$$\mu^* = \underset{x \notin P}{\text{Inf}} \ \frac{-w(x)}{d(x,P)} \ .$$

Also:

$$\mu^* = -\frac{w(z)}{d(z,P)} = \underset{i \in Iw(z)}{\text{Max}} \frac{-\langle a^i,z \rangle - b^i}{d(z,P)}$$

$$= \frac{-\langle a^i,z \rangle - b^i}{d(z,P)} \quad \forall \ i \in Iw(z)$$

$$= \underset{i \in Iw(z)}{\text{Min}} \frac{\langle a^i,x^* - z \rangle}{d(z,P)} = \mu(z) \quad .$$

From this it follows that

$$\mu^* = \mu(z) \geq \mu \quad ,$$

and as $\mu \geq \mu^*$, the theorem follows. $\|$

The proof given here is somewhat messy. One reason for its use is that it gives two new definitions of μ or μ^* in terms of directional derivatives. We will state a few related results, whose proofs are similar to, or included in, the one given above.

(i) If x is close enough to P, then

$$\langle a^i,x^*(x) - x \rangle = \langle a^j,x^*(x) - x \rangle \quad \forall \ i,j \in Iw(x) \quad .$$

This means that every extreme point of the subgradient set $\partial w(x)$ makes the same angle with the direction to the closest point to the optimal set.

(ii) Let

$$x^* \in bd \ P \qquad and \qquad i \in Iw(x^*) \quad ;$$

then

$$\partial w(x^* - \alpha a^i) = \{a^i\} \qquad \forall \alpha > 0 \quad .$$

47

Proof

$$-\alpha = a^i(x^* - \alpha a^i) + b^i \geq w(x^* - \alpha a^i)$$

$$= \underset{j\in I}{\text{Min}} \ (<a^j,x^*> + b^j - \alpha<a^j,a^i>)$$

$$\geq \underset{j\in I}{\text{Min}} \ (<a^j,x^*> + b^j) + \underset{j\in I}{\text{Min}} \ (-\alpha <a^j,a^i>)$$

$$= 0 - \alpha\underset{j\in I}{\text{Max}} \ <a^j,a^i>$$

$$= -\alpha \quad \text{as} \quad <a^j,a^i> \leq <a^i,a^i> = 1 \quad \forall j \in I \ .$$

If $a^k \neq a^i$, then

$$a^k(x^* - \alpha a^i) + b^k \geq -\alpha<a^k,a^i> > -\alpha \ ,$$

and thus $\partial w(x^* - \alpha a^i)$ contains only one element, i.e., $\{a^i\}$. ‖

This last result depends crucially upon the assumption $\|a^i\| = 1$ i I.

There is one result that is very important for subgradient optimization (for a general concave function), but which depends upon the assumption that all a^i have norm one. If we assume that an overestimate of μ is known, the only thing required to *guarantee* convergence is that an overestimate or $\mu d(x^0,P)$ be available [4].

Here it is clear that if $\tilde{w} \geq w^*$, then

$$\tilde{w} - w(x^0) \geq w^* - w(x^0) = -w(x^0) \geq \mu^*d(x^0,P) = \mu d(x^0,P) \ ,$$

and as any feasible solution to a dual problem to $\underset{x\in R^n}{\text{Max}} \ w(x)$ will provide a value $\tilde{w} \geq w^*$, it follows that $\tilde{w} - w(x^0)$ is an overestimate to $\mu d(x^0,P)$.

This is exactly the result that one would wish to extend to a general function $w(x)$. Unfortunately, given a proper definition of μ^*, this result does not extend without significant change.

Another minor result might be worth mentioning, about the quantity ν; it follows somewhat directly that if dim $P = n$ and $x^* \in$ bd P

$$\nu(C_p(x^*)) = \underset{\|e\| = 1}{\text{Max}} \quad \underset{i \in Iw(x^*)}{\text{Min}} \quad <a^i, e> \quad ,$$

and thus $\nu(C_p(x^*)) = \underset{\|e\| = 1}{\text{Max}} \quad w_1'(x^*; e)$ which could be called the intensity of the steepest ascent at x^* of the function $w_1(x)$. It also follows that

$$\nu(C_p(x^*)) = \underset{u \in \partial w_1(x^*)}{\text{Min}} \quad \|u\|$$

and thus

$$\nu = \underset{x^* \in \text{bd } P}{\text{Min}} \quad \underset{u \in \partial w_1(x^*)}{\text{Min}} \quad \|u\| \quad .$$

4. CONCLUSION

The relationship between the maximal distance relaxation method and subgradient optimization as applied to a certain function $w(x)$, whose optimal value is known, has been made explicit.

Condition numbers defined in both theories are compared; in particular $\mu = \mu^*$, so that if $\mu \leq \frac{\sqrt{2}}{2}$, then the sustainable rate of convergence for subgradient optimization is exactly equal to the rate given by the relaxation method with $\lambda = 1$.

REFERENCES

[1] Agmon, S., The Relaxation Method for Linear Inequalities, *Canadian Journal of Mathematics*, 6 (1954), 382-392.

[2] Eremin, I.I., An Iterative Method for Chebyshev Approximations of Incompatible Systems of Linear Inequalities, *Doklady Akademii Nauk SSSR*, 143 (1962), 1254-1256; *Soviet Mathematics Doklady*, 3 (1962), 570-572.

[3] Goffin, J.L., *On the Finite Convergence of the Relaxation Method for Solving Systems of Inequalities*, ORC 71-36, Operations Research Center Report, University of California, Berkeley, 1971.

[4] Goffin, J.L., On the Convergence Rates of Subgradient Optimization Methods, *Mathematical Programming*, 13, 3 (1977), 329-347.

[5] Held, M., and R.M. Karp, The Traveling-Salesman Problem and Minimum Spanning Trees: Part II, *Mathematical Programming*, 1 (1971), 6-25.

[6] Held, M., P. Wolfe, and H. Crowder, Validation of Subgradient Optimization, *Mathematical Programming*, 6, 1 (1974), 62-88.

[7] Motzkin, T., and I.J. Schoenberg, The Relaxation Method for Linear Inequalities, *Canadian Journal of Mathematics*, 6 (1954), 393-404.

[8] Oettli, W., An Iterative Method, Having Linear Rate of Convergence, for Solving a Pair of Dual Linear Programs, *Mathematical Programming*, 3 (1972), 302-311.

[9] Poljak, B.T., Minimization of Unsmooth Functionals, *Zurnal Vycislitel'noi Matematiki i Matematiceskoi Fiziki*, 9 (1969), 509-521; *USSR Computational Mathematics and Mathematical Physics*, 9, 14-29.

[10] Shor, N.Z., The Rate of Convergence of the Generalized Gradient Descent Method, *Kibernetika*, 4, 3 (1968), 98-99; *Cybernetics*, 4, 3, 79-80.

[11] Shor, N.Z., Generalized Gradient Methods for Non-Smooth Functions and Their Applications to Mathematical Programming Problems, *Ekonomika i Matematicheskie Metody*, 12, 2 (1976), 337-356 (in Russian).

AN EXTENSION OF THE METHOD OF SUBGRADIENTS*

Robin Chaney and Allen Goldstein

Until 1964, the only general method for the minimization of nondifferentiable convex functions was the so-called "cutting plane method" discovered by Cheney-Goldstein [1] and independently by Kelley [2].

In 1964, Shor [3] conceived the subgradient algorithm. Since that time, the method has been extensively developed in the Soviet Union. Some of these references are given in [3]-[12].

Lemarechal has reported at this conference that his computational experience showed that a modification of the subgradient method, due to Shor [8], was by far the most effective method for difficult nondifferentiable problems.

Generalizations of the subgradient method beyond convex functions have had partial success. The strongest result is due to Nurminskii [12]; this was corroborated by Poljak. An algorithm is formulated for a class of "weakly" convex functions. The rate of convergence obtained is slower than geometric.

The present extension of the subgradient method is to max families [13] and quasidifferentiable functions of B.N. Pshenichnyi They are useful in many problems of applied optimization.

1. ALGORITHM

1.0 Hypotheses

Let E be a real Hilbert space and f a real-valued function defined on E. Let $x \in E$ and $\varepsilon > 0$ be given. Let $B(x,\varepsilon) = \{y: \| y - x \| \le \varepsilon\}$.

---

*Supported by the National Science Foundation: MPS72-04787-A02.

51

Definition: f is called ε-*non-stationary* on B(x,ε), if for any η, 0 < η ≤ ε and for any minimizing sequence $\{x_k\}$ for f on B(x,η), $\{\|x_k - x\|\} \rightarrow$ η.

Let m(x,ε) = inf {f(y): y ∈ B(x,ε)}, T(x,ε) = {y ∈ E: f(y) ≤ m(x,ε)}, and D(x,ε) = {y: dist(y,T(x,ε)) ≤ ε}.

Assume there exist multifunctions P: D(x,ε) → subsets of T(x,ε) and φ: D(x,ε) → subsets of B(0,1). These functions, together with f, are assumed to satisfy [A], [B], and [C] below.

Assume there exist positive constants Θ, μ, and L such that whenever y ∈ D(x,ε) the following inequalities hold:

[A] $[\phi(y), y - P(y)] \geq \Theta\|y - P(y)\|$

[B] $\mu\|y - P(y)\| \leq f(y) - f(P(y)) \leq L\|y - P(y)\|$

[C] $\|y - T(x,\varepsilon)\| \leq \|y - P(y)\| \leq$

$\|y - T(x,\varepsilon)\| (1 + (\frac{\mu}{\alpha})^2)^{1/2}$, α ≥ L/Θ .

1.1 Lemma

Assume [A], [B], and [C] and the number m(x,ε) are given. Set $x_o = x, \gamma_k = [f(x_k) - f(P(x_k))]/\alpha$ and $x_{k+1} = x_k - \gamma_k\phi(x_k)$. Then $\|x_k - P(x_k)\| \leq \beta^k\|x_o - P(x_o)\|$ $0 < \beta = [1 - (\frac{\mu}{\alpha})^4]^{1/2} < 1$.

Proof: Assume $x_k \in D$. Compute $\|x_{k+1} - P(x_k)\|^2 = \|x_k - P(x_k) - \gamma_k\phi(x_k)\|^2 = \|x_k - P(x_k)\|^2 - 2\gamma_k[\phi(x_k), x_k - P(x_k)] + \gamma_k^2$. Now $[\phi(x_k), x_k - P(x_k)] \geq \Theta\|x_k - P(x_k)\| \geq \Theta[f(x_k) - f(P(x_k))]/L \geq [f(x_k) - f(P(x_k))]/\alpha_k = \gamma_k$. Hence $-2\gamma_k[\phi(x_k), x_k - P(x_k)] \leq -2\gamma_k^2$. Thus $\|x_{k+1} - P(x_{k+1})\|^2 \leq \|x_k - P(x_k)\|^2 - \gamma_k^2 =$

$\|x_k - P(x_k)\|^2 - \left(\frac{f(x_k) - f(P(x_k))}{\alpha}\right)^2 \leq \|x_k - P(x_k)\|^2 \times$

$(1 - (\frac{\mu}{\alpha})^2) \leq \|x_k - T(x,\varepsilon)\|^2 (1 - (\frac{\mu}{\alpha})^4)$. Since $\|x_{k+1} - T(x,\varepsilon)\|$ $\leq \|x_{k+1} - P(x_k)\|$ it follows that $x_{k+1} \in D(x,\varepsilon)$.

Also, $\|x_{k+1} - P(x_{k+1})\| \leq \|x_{k+1} - T(x,\varepsilon)\| (1 + (\frac{\mu}{\alpha})^2)^{1/2}$ $\leq \|x_{k+1} - P(x_k)\| (1 + (\frac{\mu}{\alpha})^2)^{1/2}$. Thus $\|x_{k+1} - P(x_{k+1})\| \leq$ $\|x_k - P(x_k)\| (1 - (\frac{\mu}{\alpha})^4)^{1/2}$.

1.2 *Definition*

By E_ε we denote the set $\{y \in E: \ f$ is ε-non-stationary on $B(y,\varepsilon)\}$.

1.3 *Theorem*

Assume f is bounded below on E, and assume [A], [B], and [C] hold for each $y \in E_\varepsilon$. A finite sequence $\{x_k\}$ can be constructed such that for some integer M, $x_M \notin E_\varepsilon$.

Proof: Observe first that by [C] inf $\{m(x,\varepsilon): \ x \in E_\varepsilon\} \geq \mu\varepsilon$. Take $x_o \in E_\varepsilon$, and let $\{x_j\}$ be the sequence constructed by the above theorem. Since $\|x_k - P(x_k)\| \downarrow 0$, we have by [B] that $\{f(x_k)\} \to m(x_o,\varepsilon)$. Again by [B], $f(x_o) - m(x_o,\varepsilon) \geq \mu\|x_o - P(x_o)\| = \mu\varepsilon$. Hence $m(x_o,\varepsilon) \leq f(x_o) - \mu\varepsilon$. Therefore for some number k_1, $f(x_{k_1}) \leq f(x_o) - \mu\varepsilon/2$. Set $x_o' = x_{k_1}$, and invoke the lemma with an ε ball around x_o' and a new mapping P' assigning points to the set $T' = x \in E$; $f(x) \leq \inf\{f(y): y \in \beta(x_o',\varepsilon)\}$. Repeating this process a sequence of numbers $f(x_{k_1}), f(x_{k_2}), \ldots$ will be generated. It follows that for some $k_s, x_{k_s} \notin E_\varepsilon$; for otherwise $\{f(x_{k_i})\} \downarrow -\infty$, contradicting that f is bounded below.

1.4 *Remarks*

In application, the number $m(x,\varepsilon)$ is in general unknown. The estimate $f(x_o) - \mu\varepsilon \geq m(x_o,\varepsilon)$ may be employed in lieu of

$m(x_o, \varepsilon)$, however. We have that $f(x_o) - \mu\varepsilon = m(x_o, \eta)$ for some η, $0 < \eta \leq \varepsilon$, and fortunately the number η is not required in the lemma or theorem. If a lower bound for the infimum of f is known, the total number of iterations to reach x_{k_s} can be estimated from 1.1.

2. APPLICATION TO SOME MAX FAMILIES OF B.N. PSHENICHNYI

2.0 General Hypotheses

Let U be a metric compactum. Assume f is defined and continuous on $E_\varepsilon \times U$, that $f(., u)$ is Gateaux differentiable on E_ε, and that

$$|f'(x, u, h) - f'(y, u, h)| \leq K\| x - y\| \ \| h \| \tag{1}$$

for all x and y in E_ε, $u \in U$ and $h \in E$. It follows that f, and F below, are locally Lipschitz on E_ε. Let

$$F(x) = \max \{f(x, u): \ u \in U\} \ , \qquad x \in E_\varepsilon \tag{2}$$

and

$$U(x) = \{u \in U: \ F(x) = f(x, u)\} \ . \tag{3}$$

The Clarke differential of F [14] is defined as

$$F^o(x, h) = \lim_{\substack{\lambda \downarrow o \\ k \to o}} \sup \left\{ \frac{F(x + k + \lambda h) - F(x + k)}{\lambda} \right\} \ .$$

The convex functional $h \to F^o(x, h)$ is the support function for a weakly compact convex set called the generalized gradient of F at x. It is denoted by $\partial F(x)$. See also [14], Propositions 1 and 2.

2.1 *Lemma*

$$\partial F(x) = \overline{co} \bigcup_{u \in U(x)} \partial f(x,u)$$

and

$$F^O(x,h) = F'_+(x,h) = \max \{f'(x,u,h): \ u \in U(x)\} \quad ,$$

where

$$F'_+(x,h) = \lim_{\lambda \to 0+} \left(\frac{F(x + \lambda h) - F(x)}{\lambda} \right)$$

Proof: By Proposition 4 (Clarke, [14]), $f'(x,u,h) = f^O(x,u,h)$.
Let $M(x) = \overline{co} \bigcup \partial f(x,u)$ and take $x \in S$ and $u \in U(x)$. Then
$F(x + \lambda h) - F(x) \geq f(x + \lambda h,u) - f(x,u)$ and so

$$\lim_{\lambda \downarrow 0} \inf \frac{F(x + \lambda h) - F(x)}{\lambda} \geq f'(x,u,h) = f^O(x,u,h)$$

$$= \max \{[\phi,h]: \ \phi \in \partial f(x,u)\} \quad .$$

Since u is arbitrary in $U(x)$,

$$F^O(x,h) \geq \lim_{\lambda \downarrow 0} \inf \frac{F(x + \lambda h) - F(x)}{\lambda}$$

$$\geq \max_{u \in U(x)} \max_{\phi \in \partial f(x,u)} [\phi,h] = \max_{\phi \in M(x)} [\phi,h] \quad .$$

(See Pshenichnyi [13], p. 166.) Hence $M(x) \subseteq \partial F(x)$. By the
definition of $F^O(x,h)$ there exist sequences $\{v_k\} \to 0$ and $\{\lambda_k\} \downarrow 0$
such that:

$$F^O(x,h) = \lim_{n \to \infty} \frac{F(x + v_n + \lambda_n h) - F(x + v_n)}{\lambda_n} \quad .$$

Choose $u_n \in U(x + v_n + \lambda_n h)$ so that

$$F(x + v_n + \lambda_n h) = f(x + v_n + \lambda_n, u_n) \quad .$$

Then

$$\frac{F(x + v_n + \lambda_n h) - F(x + v_n)}{\lambda_n} \leq \frac{f(x + v_n + \lambda_n h, u_n) - f(x + v_n, u_n)}{\lambda_n} \quad .$$

We may assume $\{u_n\} \to u^*$.

Observe that $F(x) = \lim\limits_{n \to \infty} f(x + v_n + \lambda_n h, u_n) = f(x, u^*)$; hence $u^* \in U(x)$. Therefore

$$\limsup_{\lambda \downarrow 0} \frac{F(x + \lambda h) - F(x)}{\lambda} \leq F^O(x, h)$$

$$\leq \liminf_{n \to \infty} \frac{f(x + v_n + \lambda_n h, u_n) - f(x + v_n, u_n)}{\lambda_n}$$

$$= \liminf \{ f'(x + v_n, u_n, h) + f'(\xi_n, u_n, h)$$

$$- f'(x + v_n, u_n, h) \} \leq \liminf \{ f'(x + v_n, u_n, h)$$

$$+ K\lambda_n \| h \|^2 \}$$

$$= f'(x, u^*, h) = f^O(x, u^*, h) \leq \max \{ f'(x, u, h) : \quad u \in U(x) \}$$

$$= \max_{u \in U(x)} \max_{\phi \ \partial f(x, u)} [\phi, h] = \max_{\phi \in M(x)} [\phi, h] \quad .$$

Hence

$$\partial f(x) = M(x)$$

and

$$F'_+(x, h) = F^O(x, h) = \max_{\phi \in M(x)} [\phi, h] \quad .$$

Also it is just for simplifying notations that we suppose $f_i = f(x_i)$ and $g_i \in \partial f(x_i)$. We might suppose that the user is unable to compute exactly the function and its gradient. In fact, all we have said and all we are going to say remains valid when we suppose that the user is given x_i together with some pre-scribed tolerance ε_i, and that he returns f_i and g_i such that

$$f(x_i) - \varepsilon_i \le f_i \le f(x_i) \quad \text{and} \quad g_i \in \partial_{\varepsilon_i} f(x_i) \quad .$$

Then, the only difference with the case $\varepsilon_i = 0$ is a minor modi-fication of (12). ‖

Now the question is: how do we use this bundle to compute "at best" a new point x_{k+1}, or to generate a new subgradient g_{k+1}?

From Section 1, the simplest answer is the following. Let us suppose that $G_k \subset \partial f(x_k)$; then we should choose $d_k = -Nr\ G_k$. This technique is fully justified in two cases.

(I)   When the algorithm has been stuck from
      x_1 to x_k: all the points x_i are close together
      and all the g_i's are approximately in $\partial f(x_k)$.
      Of course, this is an emergency situation: con-
      structing algorithms that we hope do not get
      stuck too often is precisely what we want to do.

(II) When the situation happens to be

      - f is quadratic and

      - all the line-searches have been exact from
         x_1 to x_k. In that case, $Nr\ G_k$ turns out to
         be the direction of conjugate gradients which
         is optimal in the sense that it points towards
         the minimum of f in the set generated by the
         bundle. Of course, this situation is not
         very interesting either: the aim of NSO is
         not to minimize quadratic functions with
         exact line-searches!

In summary, $d_k = -$ Nr G_k is a poorly justified choice, which is likely to become worse when k increases. The first idea for overcoming this has been to reset periodically, to force k to be small. This has given variants of what have come to be called *conjugate subgradient* methods.

(a) In [14], one resets as late as possible, i.e. when Nr $G_k \simeq 0$ (in which case it would be foolish to interpret it as a direction).

(b) In [5] a rather artificial observation was made: there is a simple test that detects situation (II) above, namely

$$(g_i, x_i - x_1) \leq 0 \qquad\qquad i = 1, \ldots, k \quad , \qquad\qquad (13)$$

which means that $g_i \in \partial_{\varepsilon_i} f(x_1)$, where $\varepsilon_i = f(x_1) - f(x_i)$. (In fact, equality holds in (13) when the situation is as in (II)). Accordingly, one resets whenever (13) is not met.

(c) These two rules for resetting are based on (II) above and do not seem to be very promising. More interesting are rules given in [9], directly based on (I) and on the fact that resetting leads to restart on the gradient, which is clumsy. It is better not to *reset* but to *delete* those g_i's that appear to be poor approximations of $\partial f(x_k)$. This can be done in either of the two following ways:

- delete those g_i's for which $|x_i - x_k|$ is too large, or

- define the numbers

$$\alpha_i = f(x_k) - f(x_i) - (g_i, x_k - x_i) \qquad i = 1, \ldots, k \quad , \qquad (14)$$

and delete those g_i's for which α_i is too large. (Note that $\alpha_i \geq 0$, $\alpha_k = 0$. All the information is on hand to compute α_i and there is a simple recurrence formula for computing them cheaply.) ||

The latter is very interesting because, as in Section 2, it again gives a means to measure the proximity of x_i to x_k in terms of differences in the objective. From (12) it can be seen that $g_i \in \partial_{\alpha_i} f(x_k)$. Thus, α_i measures how far g_i is from $\partial f(x_k)$. Intuitively, when computing d_k in terms of the g_i's, *the weight of g_i should be smaller when α_i is larger*.

Deletion rule (14) can be considered as a weighting of g_i by 1 if $\alpha_i \leq \delta$, 0 if $\alpha_i > \delta$, where δ is some chosen threshold. This is a tough weighting. Clearly, it would be interesting to smooth it. *We think that efficient descent methods would be obtained if this question of weighting were properly solved.* The next development tries to answer this question, probably imperfectly, as it does not eliminate the need for a threshold.

From the fact that $g_i \in \partial_{\alpha_i} f(x_k)$ $i = 1,\ldots,k$ we can write

$$\forall y \in H \ , \quad f(y) \geq f(x_k) + (g_i, y - x_k) - \alpha_i \quad i = 1,\ldots,k \ ,$$

or equivalently, by convex combination:

$$f(y) \geq f(x_k) + (\textstyle\sum \lambda_i g_i, y - x_k) - \sum \lambda_i \alpha_i$$

$$\forall \lambda: \ \lambda_i \geq 0, \qquad \sum \lambda_i = 1 \ . \qquad (15)$$

Every $y \in H$ can be described as $y = x_k + td$, $t > 0$, $|d| = 1$. In particular, if we choose $y = x_k + td$ as the next iterate, the decrement in the objective cannot be larger than the (we hope positive) number

$$\min \ \{-t(\textstyle\sum \lambda_i g_i, d) + \sum \lambda_i \alpha_i \mid \lambda_i \geq 0, \ \sum \lambda_i = 1\} \ .$$

It is therefore natural to look for the pair t and d that yields the best possible decrement, i.e. that solves

$$\max_{t>0,\,|d|=1} \quad \min_{\lambda} \; - \; t \; (\textstyle\sum \lambda_i g_i, d) \; + \; \textstyle\sum \lambda_i \alpha_i \quad . \tag{16}$$

We do not see clearly how to solve (16) (which, by the way, has no solution in general: unless $0 \in \text{conv } G_k$, t is infinite). However, parallelling with the general scheme of a descent method, we might fix t at some *guessed* value, solve (16) for d alone, and then forget (16) and perform a line-search along the *optimal* d. In that case, (16) becomes a saddle point problem in λ, d, very similar to (8); its solution is

$$\bar{d} = - \textstyle\sum \bar{\lambda}_i g_i / |\textstyle\sum \bar{\lambda}_i g_i|$$

where $\bar{\lambda}$ solves

$$\min \; |\textstyle\sum \lambda_i g_i| \; + \; \frac{1}{t} \textstyle\sum \lambda_i \alpha_i \qquad \lambda_i \geq 0, \qquad \textstyle\sum \lambda_i = 1 \quad . \tag{17}$$

(The case $\sum \bar{\lambda}_i g_i = 0$ needs finer analysis, which is not of interest here.)

Although (17) is a well-posed problem, it is not workable; but there is a trick for transforming it. $1/t$ can interpreted as the (positive) Lagrange multiplier associated with some (inequality) constraint of the form $\sum \lambda_i \alpha_i \leq \varepsilon$. To $t > 0$ given, there corresponds the right-hand side $\varepsilon = \sum \bar{\lambda}_i \alpha_i$. Since $\alpha_i \geq 0$ and $\alpha_k = 0$, the range for ε is $\varepsilon \geq 0$. Finally, because the mapping $z \rightarrow \frac{1}{2} z^2$ is monotone increasing, (17) is equivalent to

$$\begin{cases} \min \; \frac{1}{2} |\textstyle\sum \lambda_i g_i|^2 \\[2mm] \textstyle\sum \lambda_i = 1 \qquad \lambda_i \geq 0 \\[2mm] \textstyle\sum \lambda_i \alpha_i \leq \varepsilon \quad , \end{cases} \tag{18}$$

which is a simple constrained least squares problem. The paper by Mifflin in this volume is devoted to solving it.

In (17), $t = |x_{k+1} - x_k|$ is unknown. We now give an inter-
pretation of the unknown parameter ε in (18). It is convenient
to denote

$$G_k(\varepsilon) = \{g \mid g = \sum_i \lambda_i g_i, \ \sum_i \lambda_i = 1, \ \lambda_i \geq 0, \ \sum_i \lambda_i \alpha_i \leq \varepsilon\} \ .$$

It is a convex polyhedron included in G_k. Using (12), it is not
difficult to show that $G_k(\varepsilon) \subset \partial_\varepsilon f(x_k)$. Denote also $s(\varepsilon) = \sum_i \lambda_i g_i$
the optimal solution in (18). Then, $s(\varepsilon)$ defines the best hyper-
plane separating $G_k(\varepsilon)$ from the origin. If ε is very small, we
can hope that $G_k(\varepsilon)$ is a good approximation of $\partial_\varepsilon f(x_k)$, so $s(\varepsilon)$
will also separate $\partial_\varepsilon f(x_k)$ from the origin. This will guarantee
a decrease by ε in the direction $-s(\varepsilon)$, hence the need to choose
ε as large as possible. On the other hand, if ε is too large,
$G_k(\varepsilon)$ is a poor approximation and $s(\varepsilon)$ becomes meaningless in
terms of $\partial_\varepsilon f(x_k)$.

Thus, the philosophy underlying this development is a con-
struction of $\partial_\varepsilon f(x)$ for varying ε and x--instead of fixed as in
Section 2.

We can call *bundle methods* the class of methods that proceed as follows: at each iteration, consider the bundle of in-
formation $g_1, \ldots, g_k$; $\alpha_1, \ldots, \alpha_k$. Choose $\varepsilon > 0$. Solve (18) for
$s(\varepsilon)$. Make a step along $-s(\varepsilon)$. For these methods to be efficient, several questions should be solved.

Is (18) really the proper problem to solve for computing
the direction? We are supposed to find a hyperplane separating
$G_k(\varepsilon)$ from 0. However, such a hyperplane would be found also
by changing the metric, i.e. by defining some positive definite
matrix H, considering the objective $\frac{1}{2}(\sum_i \lambda_i g_i, H \sum_i \lambda_i g_i)$ in (18)
instead of $\frac{1}{2}|\sum_i \lambda_i g_i|^2$, and taking $s(\varepsilon) = H \sum_i \lambda_i g_i$ as the direc-
tion.

Second, we have not been able so far to find satisfying
automatic rules for choosing ε at each iteration. (An efficient
heuristic is $\varepsilon = \frac{1}{2}[f(x_k) - \min f]$, but it is not implementable.)

Since ε should be related to $f(x_k) - f(x_{k+1})$, a dialogue between (18) and the line-search might be necessary; this would make the direction depend on the step size, and lead to *gauche* algorithms, with *curve-searches*.

Finally, once the direction is found, we should logically move if we thus get a *sufficient* decrease. Otherwise, as in Section 2, we should add a gradient into the bundle and compute a new direction from the same x_k. How do we make the decision to move, and which gradient do we add into the bundle?

In conjugate subgradient methods, the situation is clear: one has an estimate $|d_k|^2$ of $-f'(x_k, d_k)$. One chooses $0 < m_2 < m_1 < 1$ and $\varepsilon > 0$. We look for $y = x_k + td_k$ and $g_{k+1} \in \partial f(y)$ such that

$$(g_{k+1}, d_k) \geq -m_1 |d_k|^2 \ .$$

For moving, we require in addition

$$f(y) \leq f(x_k) - m_2 t |d_k|^2 \qquad \text{(serious step: } x_{k+1} = y).$$

If this is impossible, we require

$$f(y) - t(g_{k+1}, d_k) \geq f(x_k) - \varepsilon \ \text{(null-step; } g_{k+1} \in \partial_\varepsilon f(x_k)) \ .$$

This ensures that the direction will change at the next iteration, and also that the decrease in the objective is sufficient. In bundle methods, there is no clear reason to choose the same criteria. ‖

These questions are still open.

4. RELATIONS WITH OTHER METHODS

(a) When ε approaches 0 in (18), it is clear that $s(\varepsilon)$ goes to g_k. More precisely, a bundle method with $\varepsilon = 0$ would reduce to the algorithm of Section 1.

(b) No less obviously, if ε is large enough (say $\varepsilon \geq \max \alpha_i$), $s(\varepsilon)$ is the direction of conjugate subgradients.

(c) It is also clear that (15) is just a fancy way of writing:

$$f(y) \geq f(x_i) + (g_i, y - x_i) \qquad\qquad i = 1,\ldots,k \quad,$$

which is the basis for cutting planes. A bundle method is therefore a Boxstep method [7] (or rather Ballstep, since we definitely prefer Euclidean "boxes"), i.e. the method that consists in minimizing the linearization $\bar{f}$ of f inside a ball around x_k, and then extrapolating by some line-search. In such a method, the size of the ball is t in (17), and we are now going to make clear its relation with ε in (18).

First of all, $s(\varepsilon) = 0$ corresponds to the case where the minimum of $\bar{f}$ is attained in the interior of the ball. In that case, we have an optimality condition $f(x_k) \leq \min f + \varepsilon$ (since $s(\varepsilon) = 0 \in \partial_\varepsilon f(x_k)$); on the other hand, ballstep is then equivalent to the pure cutting plane, and solving the linear program without a normalization constraint also provides an underestimate on min f.

Suppose now the typical situation $s(\varepsilon) \neq 0$. Let $u \geq 0$ be the Lagrange multiplier of the extra constraint $\sum \lambda_i \alpha_i \leq \varepsilon$ in (18). Then

$$u = - \frac{d}{d\varepsilon} (\tfrac{1}{2}|s(\varepsilon)|^2) = - |s(\varepsilon)| \frac{d}{d\varepsilon} (|s(\varepsilon)|) \quad.$$

Now consider (17); set $\varepsilon = \sum \bar{\lambda}_i \alpha_i$. There also

$$\frac{1}{t} = - \frac{d}{d\varepsilon} (|\sum \bar{\lambda}_i g_i|) \quad.$$

From the equivalence between (17) and (18), we know that $\sum \bar{\lambda}_i g_i = s(\varepsilon)$. Therefore $\frac{1}{t} = - \frac{d}{d\varepsilon} (|s(\varepsilon)|)$ and we have the basic relation

$$ut = |s(\varepsilon)| \quad. \qquad\qquad\qquad\qquad (19)$$

In ballstep, the minimum of the linearization $\bar{f}$ of f is
attained at $\bar{x} = x_k + t\bar{d}$ (provided the ball constraint is active)
where $\bar{d}$, of norm 1, is given a posteriori by $\bar{d} = -s(\varepsilon)/|s(\varepsilon)|$.
Therefore, after having solved (18), we can say that, if the
ballstep problem had been solved with a ball size $t = s(\varepsilon)|/u$,
one would have obtained the point

$$\bar{x} = x_k + t\bar{d} = x_k + \frac{|s(\varepsilon)|}{u} \times (-s(\varepsilon)/|s(\varepsilon)|) = x_k - \frac{1}{u} s(\varepsilon) \quad .$$

In particular, when $\varepsilon \to +\infty$, $u \to 0$. From (19), if $0 \notin \text{conv } G_k$,
$t \to +\infty$. We can interpret this result by saying: when $0 \notin \text{conv } G_k$,
the pure cutting plane problem is unbounded. There is one (in-
finite) solution--namely the limit of solutions of cutting plane
problems bounded with the Euclidean norm--which gives the con-
jugate subgradient direction (since $s(\varepsilon) = \text{Nr } G_k$ when $u = 0$).

On the other hand, when $\varepsilon \to 0$, u goes to some finite value,
i.e. t does not go to 0. This means that there is a strictly
positive t_0 such that the ballstep direction is that of steepest
descent whenever the ball size is smaller than t_0. (This was
observed in [7]).

(d) Consider the case where the function to be minimized
has the form

$$f(x) = \max_i h_i(x) \quad .$$

In this volume, Pshenichnyi gives an algorithm in which the
direction d_k solves the problem

$$\begin{cases} \min_{\eta,d} \quad \eta + \tfrac{1}{2}K|d|^2 \\ \\ (\nabla h_i(x_k),d) + h_i(x_k) \leq \eta \qquad i \text{ such that} \\ \qquad\qquad\qquad\qquad\qquad\qquad h_i(x_k) \geq f(x_k) - \delta \end{cases} \qquad (20)$$

for some positive constants K and δ (strictly speaking, he chooses K = 1, but it is more convenient for our development to allow for different values).

Since, at the optimum of (20), there is at least one active constraint, we can replace η by $\max_i [(\nabla h_i(x_k),d) + h_i(x_k)]$ and solve instead of (20):

$$\min_d \tfrac{1}{2}K|d|^2 + \max \{\nabla h_i(x_k),d) + h_i(x_k) \mid i \text{ such that }$$
$$h_i(x_k) \geq f(x_k) - \delta\} \ .$$

Using the same convexification technique as in (16)-(17), we see that in fact (20) is solved by

$$\bar{d} = -\frac{1}{K} \sum_i \bar{\lambda}_i \nabla h_i(x_k) \qquad \text{where } \bar{\lambda} \text{ solves}$$

$$\min \tfrac{1}{2}|\sum \lambda_i \nabla h_i(x_k)|^2 - K \sum \lambda_i h_i(x_k) \qquad \lambda_i \geq 0, \ \sum \lambda_i = 1 \ . \quad (21)$$

Again K can be considered as the (positive) Lagrange multiplier associated with some (inequality) constraint of the form $\sum_i \lambda_i h_i(x_k) \geq \beta$; this shows a strong relation with (17) and (18). We now make this relation more precise: any convex function f(x) may be represented as

$$f(x) = \sup_{y,g\in\partial f(y)} f(y) + (g,x - y) \ .$$

Therefore, any convex minimization problem is equivalent to

$$\begin{cases} \min\limits_{v,x} \quad v \\[2mm] f(y) + (g,x - y) \leq v \qquad \forall y \in H, \qquad \forall g \in \partial f(y) \ , \end{cases} \quad (22)$$

i.e. some sort of linear programming problem; of course this is highly criticizable since (22) contains an infinite number of constraints which, in addition, are not explicitly known. However, one could think of a method of constraint accumulation, in which one would replace (22) by the relaxed problem

$$\min_{v,x} \quad v$$

$$f_i + (g_i, x - x_i) \leq v \qquad i = 1,\ldots,k \quad ,$$

where x_i, f_i, g_i make up the bundle of Section 3.

Analogously with the present situation, we can set

$$h_i(x) = f_i + (g_i, x - x_i) \quad , \qquad\qquad \nabla h_i(x) = g_i \quad .$$

We then observe that

$$h_i(x_k) = f(x_k) - \alpha_i \qquad\qquad (\alpha_i \text{ defined in (14)}) \quad .$$

Therefore (21) takes the form

$$\min \tfrac{1}{2} |\textstyle\sum_i \lambda_i g_i|^2 \quad \sum_i \lambda_i = 1, \quad \lambda_i \geq 0, \quad \sum_i \lambda_i [f(x_k) - \alpha_i] \geq \beta \quad ,$$

and the equivalence with (18) is established by taking $\beta = f(x_k) - \varepsilon$, so that K in (20) is u in (18).

The role of δ in (20) is to neglect the subgradients for which α_i is too large, i.e., it is exactly the deletion rule Section 3(c) of Mifflin.

Observe in particular that when $K = 0$ in (21), $\varepsilon = +\infty$ in (18). Then the direction of Pshenichnyi is that of Demjanov [2]. In other words, Mifflin's version of conjugate subgradients is a variant of Demjanov's method, in which one computes not the values $h_i(x_k)$ that make up $f(x_k)$, but rather the values at x_k of the linearized f at previous x_i (this has been pointed out to us by Bertsekas in a private communication). Although (21) with $K \neq 0$ is apparently only a slight modification of Demjanov (at least when δ is small, since one has $f(x_k) - \delta \leq h_i(x_k) \leq f(x_k)$), taking the differences in $h_i(x_k)$ into account is a refinement.

(e)   It is rather amusing to see that such a refinement has existed for quite some time in a slightly different context: Consider an ordinary mathematical programming problem,

$$\min\ f(x)$$

$$c_j(x) \leq 0 \qquad j = 1,\ldots,m \ .$$

(23)

Many methods for solving it are based on the principle of feasible directions.   In their original form, presented by Zoutendijk [15], they consisted in solving at each iteration the problem

$$
\left\{
\begin{array}{l}
\min_{\eta,d} \quad \eta \\[2ex]
(\nabla f(x_k),d) \leq \eta \\[2ex]
\theta_j(\nabla c_j(x_k),d) \leq \eta \quad j \text{ in some suitable subset of } \{1,\ldots m\} \\[2ex]
d \text{ in some suitable normalization set.}
\end{array}
\right.
$$

(24)

It is certainly numerically necessary to introduce the weights θ_j, since there is no reason to compare variations in the constraints with variations in the objective, even if one admits that the user himself has scaled the space H to strive to homogenize variations in the objective alone. ||

As with (20), this problem can be transformed to look like (21).   Since the values of the constraints $c_j(x_k)$ are neglected in (24), we would get (21) with K = 0, i.e. some Demjanov or conjugate subgradient method.   It would therefore be better to consider in (24) the constraints

$$\theta_j[c_j(x_k) + (\nabla c_j(x_k),d)] \leq \eta \ .$$

This has been done by Zoutendijk [15] himself, and (with $\theta_j \equiv 1$) by Topkis & Veinott [13], Pironneau & Polak [10] and Mangasarian

[6]. If, as is often true, the $c_j(x_k)$ are slightly negative numbers, the difference is little, but, from the analysis of rates of convergence in [10], the trick is really helpful (as is the use of Euclidean norm, as shown in the same paper). Correspondingly, the algorithm of Pshenichnyi for solving (23) (see his paper in this volume) introduces the same trick. (In addition, it is more satisfactory, since it does not need x_k to be feasible.)

To sum up this Section, (22) establishes a link between non-differentiable optimization and nonlinear programming. A non-smooth problem is a linear program with an infinite number of noncomputable constraints. To solve it, one could take advantage of the large amount of work done in nonlinear programming. Conversely, any efficient method of NSO could help in studying the (unsolved) general problem of nonlinear programming (23); for the latter, the theory of ε-subgradients is an apparently new and promising tool.

Most of the methods existing both in NSO and in NLP are essentially equivalent, provided the parameters they generally contain are carefully updated.

Through (12), the theory of ε-subgradients seems to shed some light on the fundamental question of scaling the space. It has been observed that the best numerical results are often obtained by quasi-Newton methods and Shor's method of dilatation of the space along differences of gradients [12]. Both these methods (heuristic in NSO) define at each iteration a metric H_k, assumed also to scale the variables. However, the formulae for updating H_k are *off-line* (in particular they do not involve values of the objective). It would probably be important to know what kind of relationship exists between ε-subgradients (i.e. general NLP), quasi-Newton methods, and Shor's methods.

REFERENCES

[1] Clarke, F.H., Generalized Gradients and Applications,
     Trans. of the Am. Math. Soc., 205 (1975), 247-262.

[2] Demjanov, V.F., Algorithms for Some Minimax Problems,
     Journal of Computation and Systems Sciences, 2 (1968),
     342-380.

[3] Goldstein, A.A., Optimization of Lipschitz Continuous
     Functions, *Mathematical Programming*, 13, 1 (1977),
     14-22.

[4] Lemarechal, C., An Algorithm for Minimizing Convex Func-
     tions, in J.L. Rosenfeld, ed., *Information Processing
     '74*, North-Holland, Amsterdam, 1974.

[5] Lemarechal, C., An Extension of Davidon Methods to Non-
     differentiable Problems, in M.L. Balinski and P. Wolfe,
     eds., *Nondifferentiable Optimization*, Mathematical
     Programming Study 3, North-Holland, Amsterdam, 1975.

[6] Mangasarian, O.L., Dual, Feasible Direction Algorithms, in
     A.V. Balakrishnan, ed., *Techniques of Optimization*,
     Academic Press, New York, 1972.

[7] Marsten, R.E., W.W. Hogan, and J.W. Blankenship, The Box-
     step Method for Large-Scale Optimization, *Operations
     Research*, 23, 3 (1975), 389-405.

[8] Mifflin, R., Semi-Smooth and Semi-Convex Functions in Con-
     strained Optimization, *SIAM Journal on Control and
     Optimization*, 15, 6 (1977).

[9] Mifflin, R., An Algorithm for Constrained Optimization
     with Semi-Smooth Functions, *Mathematics of Operations
     Research*, 2, 2 (1977), 191-207.

[10] Pironneau, O., and E. Polak, Rate of Convergence of a Class
     of Methods of Feasible Directions, *SIAM Journal on
     Numerical Analysis*, 10, 1 (1973).

[11] Rockafellar, R.T., *Convex Analysis*, Princeton University
     Press, Princeton, N.J., 1970.

[12] Shor, N.Z., and L.P. Shabashova, On the Solution of Mini-
     max Problems by the Generalized Gradient Method with
     Space Dilatation, *Kibernetika*, No. 1 (1972).

[13] Topkis, D.M., and A.F. Veinott, On the Convergence of Some
     Feasible Direction Algorithms for Nonlinear Program-
     ming, *SIAM Journal on Control*, 5, 2 (1967), 268-279.

[14]   Wolfe, P., A Method of Conjugate Subgradients for Minimiz-
       ing Nondifferentiable Functions, in M.L. Balinski
       and P. Wolfe, eds., *Nondifferentiable Optimization*,
       Mathematical Programming Study 3, North-Holland,
       Amsterdam, 1975.

[15]   Zoutendijk, G., *Methods of Feasible Directions*, Elsevier,
       Amsterdam, 1960.

A FEASIBLE DESCENT ALGORITHM FOR LINEARLY CONSTRAINED LEAST SQUARES PROBLEMS

Robert Mifflin

1. INTRODUCTION

Consider the *constrained least squares problem* of finding an n-vector $x = (x_1, x_2, \ldots, x_n)^T$ to

$$\text{minimize} \quad \tfrac{1}{2}|Px - c|^2 = \tfrac{1}{2}x^T P^T Px - c^T Px + \tfrac{1}{2}c^T c$$

$$\text{subject to} \quad Ax = b$$

$$x \geq 0$$

where P is a p × n matrix, c is a p-vector, A is an m × n matrix, b is an m-vector and a superscript T denotes transposition. The column rank of P may be less than n. We give a numerically stable method for solving this problem based on one given by Wolfe [6] for the special case where c = 0, m = 1, every component of the row vector A is 1 and b =1. The algorithm solves a sequence of reduced dimension subproblems without nonnegativity constraints. The method is similar in philosophy to one given by Stoer [5], but our procedure for solving the subproblems, which is inspired by the work of Golub and Saunders [2], is different. The algorithm handles equality constraints directly; i.e., we do not use them to eliminate variables and then create inequality constraints from the corresponding nonnegativity restrictions as is suggested by Lawson and Hanson [3] in order to apply their procedure for inequality constrained problems, which involves yet another problem transformation.

We note that general quadratic programming algorithms may be applied to this problem, but, if they do not exploit the factorized structure of the Hessian matrix P^TP to deal with its possible singularity (or near singularity), such methods may fail.

Our method can also be used to solve strictly convex quadratic programming problems by transforming the objective function as shown in [2, p. 248]. Inequality constraints may be handled by introducing nonnegative slack or surplus variables. To modify the algorithm to deal with variables x_i that are not restricted to be nonnegative, one only needs to work out the implications of expressing such a variable as the difference of two nonnegative variables.

This study was motivated by the fact that Lemarechal's [4] numerical algorithm for minimizing a nondifferentiable function needs a numerically stable subroutine for solving the special constrained least squares problem where

$$n \geq 2 \quad, \qquad m = 2 \quad, \qquad c = 0 \quad,$$

$$A = \begin{bmatrix} 1 & \alpha_1 & \alpha_2 & \cdots & \alpha_{n-1} \\ 0 & 1 & 1 & \cdots & 1 \end{bmatrix} \quad, \qquad b = \begin{bmatrix} \varepsilon \\ 1 \end{bmatrix} \quad,$$

$$\alpha_i \geq 0 \quad \text{for } i = 1,2,\ldots,n-1 \quad, \qquad \alpha_1 < \varepsilon \quad,$$

and

$$P = \begin{bmatrix} 0 \\ 0 \\ \vdots \\ 0 \end{bmatrix} \quad g_1 \quad g_2 \quad \cdots \quad g_{n-1} \end{bmatrix} \quad.$$

In this application the p-vectors $g_1, g_2, \ldots, g_{n-1}$ are generalized gradients of a function of p variables to be minimized, and the solution method employed must not require these vectors to be linearly independent.

2. THE ALGORITHM

For a matrix B we denote its ith row by B_i and its jth column by B^j. Thus, $B^j = B^T{}_j$. For a vector $y = (y_1, y_2, \ldots, y_\ell)^T$, $y > 0$ means $y_i > 0$ for each $i = 1, 2, \ldots, \ell$.

For x to be an optimal solution to the above constrained least squares problem it is both necessary and sufficient (because of objective convexity and constraint linearity) that x and some m-vector u satisfy the *optimality conditions*:

$$Ax = b$$

$$x \geq 0$$

$$A^T u + P^T (Px - c) \geq 0$$

$$A^T{}_j u + P^T{}_j (Px - c) = 0 \quad \text{or} \quad x_j = 0 \quad \text{for each } j = 1, 2, \ldots, n \quad .$$

Throughout, $J \subseteq \{1, 2, \ldots, n\}$ denotes a nonempty set of column indices corresponding to a nonvacuous submatrix $\begin{bmatrix} B \\ Q \end{bmatrix}$ of columns of $\begin{bmatrix} A \\ P \end{bmatrix}$; i.e.,

$$j \in J \quad \text{if and only if} \quad \begin{bmatrix} A^j \\ P^j \end{bmatrix} \text{ is a column of } \begin{bmatrix} B \\ Q \end{bmatrix} \quad .$$

Each submatrix generated by the algorithm satisfies the assumption that

$$\begin{bmatrix} B \\ Q \end{bmatrix} \quad \text{has full column rank} \quad . \tag{A1}$$

For each such matrix we require a solution (y, u) to the corresponding linear system

$$By = b \tag{1a}$$

$$B^T u + Q^T Q y = Q^T c \quad . \tag{1b}$$

A solution procedure is given in Section 3 for the *nondegenerate case* when

B has full row rank . (A2)

This type of assumption is also made in [5]. For the special problem with m = 1 in [6], (A2) is always satisfied. For the case when (A2) does not hold, a degeneracy resolving procedure that takes into account possible nonuniqueness of u has been worked out by the author. This procedure may appear in a subsequent paper.

The following sequence of lemmas serves to motivate the algorithm. All proofs are deferred to the last section of this paper.

Lemma 1

Suppose (A1) holds. If (1) has a solution then y is unique. Furthermore, if (A2) also holds then (1) has a unique solution (y,u) and the solution procedure of Section 3 finds it.

Remark

For the case when (A2) does not hold, the solution procedure can be modified to determine whether or not (1) has a solution, and in the former case to find y and the associated u-set. It can be shown that if (A1) holds and there exists a vector $\bar{y}$ such that $B\bar{y} = b$, then (1) has a solution.

Lemma 2

(y,u) solves (1) if and only if y minimizes $|Qy - c|^2$ subject to By = b. In this case

$$|Qy - c|^2 = -b^T u - c^T (Qy - c) .$$ (2)

Lemma 3

Suppose (y,u) solves (1). Define a corresponding n-vector x by

$$x_j = \begin{cases} y_j & \text{if } j \in J \\ 0 & \text{if } j \notin J \end{cases}$$

where J corresponds to $\begin{bmatrix} B \\ Q \end{bmatrix}$ as defined above. If

$$y \geq 0$$

and

$$A^T_j u + P^T_j (Qy - c) \geq 0 \qquad \text{for all } j \notin J , \tag{3}$$

then x and u satisfy the optimality conditions and, hence, x is an optimal solution to the constrained least squares problem.

Remark

For the special problem of Section 1 with $m = 2$ and $u = (u_1, u_2)^T$, (2) becomes

$$|Qy|^2 = -\varepsilon u_1 - u_2$$

and the left-hand side of (3) becomes

$$u_1 \qquad\qquad\qquad \text{if } j = 1$$

or

$$\alpha_{j-1} u_1 + u_2 + g^T_{j-1} Qy \qquad \text{if } j \geq 2 .$$

Lemma 4

Suppose (A1) holds and (y,u) solves (1). If

$$A^T_\ell u + P^T_\ell (Qy - c) < 0 \qquad \text{for some } \ell \notin J \tag{4}$$

then $\begin{bmatrix} B & A^\ell \\ Q & P^\ell \end{bmatrix}$ has full column rank.

Remark

Note that if B has full row rank then so does $[B \ A^\ell]$. Thus, by Lemma 4, if (A1) and (A2) hold for $\begin{bmatrix} B \\ Q \end{bmatrix}$ and B, respectively, then they hold for the augmented matrices $\begin{bmatrix} B & A^\ell \\ Q & P^\ell \end{bmatrix}$ and $[B \ A^\ell]$.

These augmented matrices correspond to the augmented linear system

$$By^+ + A^\ell y^+_\ell = b \tag{1a$^+$}$$

$$B^T u^+ + Q^T(Qy^+ + P^\ell y^+_\ell) = Q^T c \tag{1b$^+$}$$

$$A^T_\ell u^+ + P^T_\ell (Qy^+ + P^\ell y^+_\ell) = P^T_\ell c \ . \tag{1c$^+$}$$

Lemma 5

Suppose (A1) and (A2) hold, (y,u) solves (1), and (4) holds. Then (1)$^+$ has a solution (y^+, y^+_ℓ, u^+) such that

$$y^+_\ell > 0$$

and

$$|Qy^+ + P^\ell y^+_\ell - c|^2 - |Qy - c|^2 = y^+_\ell \left(A^T_\ell u + P^T_\ell (Qy - c) \right) < 0 \ . \tag{5}$$

Lemma 6

Suppose that the assumptions of Lemma 5 hold and that $y > 0$. Let $\bar{\lambda}$ be the largest value of $\lambda \in [0,1]$ such that

$$\lambda \begin{bmatrix} y_j^+ \\ y_\ell^+ \end{bmatrix} + (1 - \lambda) \begin{bmatrix} y \\ 0 \end{bmatrix} \geqq 0 \quad .$$

Define the $|J| + 1$ vector z by

$$z_j = \begin{cases} \bar{\lambda} y_j^+ + (1 - \bar{\lambda}) y_j & \text{for } j \in J \\ \bar{\lambda} y_\ell^+ & \text{for } j = \ell \quad . \end{cases}$$

Then $\bar{\lambda} > 0$, $z_\ell > 0$, $z \geqq 0$,

$$[B \quad A^\ell] z = b \tag{6}$$

and

$$|[Q \quad P^\ell] z - c|^2 < |Qy - c|^2 \quad . \tag{7}$$

Furthermore, if $y^+ > 0$, then $\bar{\lambda} = 1$ and $z = \begin{bmatrix} y^+ \\ y_\ell^+ \end{bmatrix} > 0$, or if $y^+ \not> 0$ then $z_k = 0$ for some $k \in J$.

To initiate the algorithm we assume that we have an index set J and a corresponding full column rank matrix $\begin{bmatrix} B \\ Q \end{bmatrix}$ such that (1) has a solution with $y > 0$. See Section 5 for an initialization phase that will either provide this initial condition or indicate its infeasibility. Given this initial condition, the algorithm is as follows.

Step 1   Solve (1) for (y, u).
          If $y > 0$ go to Step 2. Otherwise go to Step 3.

Step 2   Test the validity of (3).
          If (3) holds stop. Otherwise ((4) holds) set $\bar{y}_i = y_i$ for each $i \in J$ and $\bar{y}_\ell = 0$, append index ℓ to J and column $\begin{bmatrix} A^\ell \\ P^\ell \end{bmatrix}$ to $\begin{bmatrix} B \\ Q \end{bmatrix}$, and go to Step 1.

Step 3   Let $\bar{\lambda}$ be the maximum value of $\lambda \in [0,1]$ such that
$$\lambda y + (1 - \lambda)\bar{y} \geq 0$$
and set
$$z = \bar{\lambda}y + (1 - \bar{\lambda})\bar{y} \quad .$$
For each i such that $z_i > 0$, set $\bar{y}_i = z_i$, and for
each k such that $z_k = 0$, delete index k from J and
the corresponding column $\begin{bmatrix} A^k \\ P^k \end{bmatrix}$ from $\begin{bmatrix} B \\ Q \end{bmatrix}$ and go to
Step 1.

We now show that the algorithm is well defined.

Because of the initialization condition the first subproblem
(1) to be solved has a solution $y > 0$, and therefore Step 2 is
executed before Step 3, so $\bar{y}$ is properly initialized to a non-
negative-valued vector.

At each execution of Step 2, if the stop does not occur, a
new index ℓ is added to J satisfying (4) and $\bar{y}$ and B are updated
such that $\bar{y} \geq 0$ and $B\bar{y} = b$. From Lemma 4 and the remark following
Lemma 1 the new system (1) will have a solution.

When entering Step 3 we have J, $y \nmid 0$ and $\bar{y}$. By the updating
in Steps 2 and 3, $\bar{y} \geq 0$. Therefore, there exists a $\lambda \in [0,1]$ such
that $\lambda y + (1 - \lambda)\bar{y} \geq 0$ (for example $\lambda = 0$). From the definitions
of $\bar{\lambda}$ and z, there exists $k \in J$ such that $z_k = 0$. Hence, at least
index k is deleted from J. A new J and a new $\bar{y} > 0$ are defined.
Lemma 7, in particular, ensures that the new J is not empty and
that the new system (1) has a solution. This lemma deals with the
situation after an execution of Step 3 in terms of data at the
most recent execution of Step 2.

Lemma 7

Suppose at Step 3 we have $\begin{bmatrix} B \\ Q \end{bmatrix}$ satisfying (A1), and

$$
\text{(H)} \begin{cases}
z \geqq 0 \quad , \\[2ex]
Bz = b \quad , \\[2ex]
z_{\ell^\circ} > 0 \quad , \\[2ex]
z_k = 0 \quad \text{for some } k \neq \ell^\circ \quad ; \\[2ex]
|Qz - c|^2 < |Q^\circ y^\circ - c|^2
\end{cases}
$$

where, at the most recent execution of Step 2, J°, B°, Q° and y° were the entering values of J, B, Q and y, and ℓ° was the index added to J°. Let the new values of J, B and Q defined at Step 3 be denoted J^-, B^- and Q^-, respectively. Then the new system (1) has a solution $y = y^-$ such that either

$$
y^- > 0 \quad \text{and} \quad |Q^- y^- - c|^2 < |Q^\circ y^\circ - c|^2 \tag{8}
$$

or $y^- \ngtr 0$ and the above hypotheses (H) are satisfied with $z = z^-$, $B = B^-$ and $Q = Q^-$ where z^- is the value of z determined at the next execution of Step 3.

By recursive application of Lemmas 1 through 7 it is now not difficult to establish finite convergence of the algorithm.

Theorem

Suppose the initial condition holds and (A2) holds for each matrix B generated by the algorithm. Then after a finite number of executions of Steps 1, 2 and 3, the algorithm terminates with an optimal solution to the constrained least squares problem.

Proof

To each J considered at Step 1 there corresponds a unique y solution of (1) and a corresponding *objective value* $\frac{1}{2}|Qy - c|^2 = \frac{1}{2}|Px - c|^2$ where x is the n-vector defined by appending zeros to y as in Lemma 3.

We now show that each entry to Step 2 has an associated objective value that is strictly lower than the one at the previous entry to Step 2, and, furthermore, that the number of consecutive executions of Step 3 between Step 2 executions is finite.

By Lemma 6, the above statement is clearly true if there are no intermediate Step 3 executions. So suppose Step 3 is entered after some execution of Step 2 which adds index $\ell°$ to J. By Lemma 6 we have at this first entry to Step 3 that the hypotheses (H) of Lemma 7 are satisfied. From Lemma 7, for all subsequent consecutive executions of Step 3 we have $z_{\ell°} > 0$ and some index $k \neq \ell°$ is removed from J. Therefore, J never becomes empty, the number of such consecutive Step 3 executions is finite, and furthermore, by Lemma 7, this sequence must terminate with (8) being satisfied. Now (8) implies a return to Step 2 with a strictly improved objective value.

Now, since the number of possible index sets J is finite and all such sets corresponding to entries to Step 2 must be distinct (due to their different corresponding objective values), the algorithm is finite.

3. SOLUTION PROCEDURE FOR (1)

Suppose (A1) and (A2) hold and $\begin{bmatrix} B \\ Q \end{bmatrix}$ has q columns. Let R be an upper triangular nonsingular $q \times q$ matrix such that

$$[B^T Q^T] \begin{bmatrix} B \\ Q \end{bmatrix} = R^T R \quad , \tag{9}$$

and let W be a $q \times m$ matrix such that

$$R^T W = B^T \quad , \tag{10}$$

ω be a q-vector such that

$$R^T \omega = Q^T c \quad , \tag{11}$$

and S be an upper triangular nonsingular m × m matrix such that

$$W^T W = S^T S \quad .$$ (12)

R and S can be found by orthogonal factorization (see, for example, [1,2,3,5]) of $\begin{bmatrix} B \\ Q \end{bmatrix}$ and W, respectively, which is possible by the full rank assumptions (A1) and (A2). See Section 5 for simple determinations of R, W, ω and S in some special cases and see the next section for updating these quantities when $\begin{bmatrix} B \\ Q \end{bmatrix}$ is changed. Having R, W, ω and S, the solution procedure is as follows:

Solve the triangular linear system

$$S^T w = b - W^T \omega$$

for w, and then solve the triangular linear system

$$Sv = w$$

for v so that v satisfies

$$S^T Sv = b - W^T \omega \quad .$$ (13)

Then set

$$u = b - v$$ (14)

and solve the triangular linear system

$$Ry = Wv + \omega$$ (15)

for y.

4. UPDATING

To perform the updating of R, W, ω and S we require a transformation that can take a 2-vector

$$\begin{bmatrix} z_1 \\ z_2 \end{bmatrix} \quad \text{into} \quad \gamma \begin{bmatrix} 1 \\ 0 \end{bmatrix}$$

where

$$\gamma^2 = z_1^2 + z_2^2 \quad .$$

This Euclidean norm-preserving transformation can be accomplished by multiplying $\begin{bmatrix} z_1 \\ z_2 \end{bmatrix}$ on the left by a *Givens matrix*

$$G = \begin{bmatrix} c & s \\ s & -c \end{bmatrix}$$

where

$$\gamma = \text{sign}(z_1) \left(z_1^2 + z_2^2 \right)^{\frac{1}{2}} \quad ,$$

$$c = z_1/\gamma \quad ,$$

$$s = z_2/\gamma \quad ,$$

and the convention for $z_1 = 0$ is that $\gamma = z_2$, $c = 0$ and $s = 1$. Note that $G^T = G^{-1}$, i.e. G is an *orthogonal* matrix. See Gill, Golub, Murray and Saunders [1] for details concerning properties and uses of Givens transformations in connection with orthogonal factorization.

Augmentation

When $\begin{bmatrix} B \\ Q \end{bmatrix}$ is replaced at Step 2 by $\begin{bmatrix} B & A^\ell \\ Q & P^\ell \end{bmatrix}$, replace

$$R \text{ by } \begin{bmatrix} R & r \\ 0 & \rho \end{bmatrix} \quad ,$$

W by $\begin{bmatrix} W \\ \bar{W} \end{bmatrix}$,

ω by $\begin{bmatrix} \omega \\ \bar{\omega} \end{bmatrix}$,

S by $\bar{S}$,

where r solves

$$R^T r = B^T A^{\ell} + Q^T P^{\ell} \ ,$$

$$\rho = \left(|A^{\ell}|^2 + |P^{\ell}|^2 - |r|^2 \right)^{\frac{1}{2}} \ ,$$

$$\bar{w} = (A^T_{\ell} - r^T W)/\rho \ ,$$

$$\bar{\omega} = (P^T_{\ell} c - r^T \omega)/\rho \ ,$$

and $\bar{S}$ is determined as in [1, pp. 529-530] as follows.

Apply appropriate 2 × 2 Givens transformations sequentially for i = 1,2,...,m to rows i and m + 1 of

$$\begin{bmatrix} S \\ \bar{w} \end{bmatrix}$$

to reduce $\bar{w}$ to the zero vector and obtain

$$\begin{bmatrix} \bar{S} \\ 0 \end{bmatrix}$$

where $\bar{S}$ is upper triangular.

The validity of these replacements may be established by making the appropriate multiplications and using the fact that a sequence of Givens transformations is equivalent to multiplication by an orthogonal matrix.

Deletion

When the kth column of the q column matrix $\begin{bmatrix} B \\ Q \end{bmatrix}$ is deleted
at Step 3 replace R, W, ω and S by $\bar{R}$, $\bar{W}$, $\bar{\omega}$ and $\bar{S}$, respectively,
where the latter quantities are determined as follows.

As in [1, pp. 533-534], apply appropriate 2 × 2 Givens transformations sequentially for i = k,k+1,...,q-1 to rows i and i + 1
of

$$[R^1 R^2 ... R^{k-1} R^{k+1} ... R^q \ W \ \omega]$$

to form

$$\begin{bmatrix} \bar{R} & \bar{W} & \bar{\omega} \\ 0 & \underline{w} & \underline{\omega} \end{bmatrix}$$

where

$\bar{R}$ is a q-1 × q-1 upper triangular matrix,
$[\bar{W} \ \bar{\omega}]$ is q-1 × m+1,
and ($\underline{w} \ \underline{\omega}$) is 1 × m+1 .

Then, as in [1, pp. 530-531], solve the triangular linear
system

$$S^T s = \underline{w}^T \ ;$$

for s, set

$$\delta = \left(1 - |s|^2 \right)^{\frac{1}{2}} \ ;$$

and apply appropriate 2 × 2 Givens transformations sequentially
for i = m,m-1,...,1 to rows i and m + 1 of

$$\begin{bmatrix} s & S \\ \delta & 0 \end{bmatrix}$$

to reduce s to the zero vector and form

$$\begin{bmatrix} 0 & \bar{S} \\ 1 & s^T \end{bmatrix}$$

where $\bar{S}$ is upper triangular, and the expression for the bottom row, as well as the validity of $\bar{R}$, $\bar{W}$, $\bar{\omega}$ and $\bar{S}$, follows from the orthogonality of Givens transformations.

5. INITIALIZATION

For the special problem with m = 2 given in Section 1, a starting matrix is

$$\begin{bmatrix} B \\ Q \end{bmatrix} = \begin{bmatrix} 1 & \alpha_1 \\ 0 & 1 \\ 0 & g_1 \end{bmatrix}$$

for which

$$R = \begin{bmatrix} 1 & \alpha_1 \\ 0 & (1 + |g_1|^2)^{\frac{1}{2}} \end{bmatrix}$$

$$W = S = \begin{bmatrix} 1 & 0 \\ 0 & (1 + |g_1|^2)^{-\frac{1}{2}} \end{bmatrix} \quad , \quad \omega = 0$$

and

$$y = \begin{bmatrix} \varepsilon - \alpha_1 \\ 1 \end{bmatrix} > 0 \quad .$$

For the general problem, if a starting matrix is not available we can first solve the initialization problem of minimizing $\left| [-b \ A] \begin{bmatrix} t \\ x \end{bmatrix} \right|^2$

subject to $t = 1$

$t, x \geq 0$.

For this problem a starting matrix is

$$\begin{bmatrix} B \\ Q \end{bmatrix} = \begin{bmatrix} 1 \\ -b \end{bmatrix}$$

for which

$$R = W^{-1} = S^{-1} = \left(1 + |b|^2\right)^{\frac{1}{2}} , \qquad \omega = 0 \text{ and } y = 1 .$$

Note that this initialization problem is never degenerate, since all row vectors B generated must contain the coefficient 1 corresponding to variable t. Our algorithm applied to this special initialization problem is essentially that of Lawson and Hanson [3, p. 161] for the problem of minimizing $|Ax - b|^2$ subject to $x \geq 0$.

If the optimal value of the initialization problem is positive then the constrained least squares problem has no feasible solution. Suppose this optimal value is zero. Then the corresponding optimal x satisfies $x \geq 0$ and $Ax = b$. If $x \neq 0$ the set of columns A^j for which $x_j > 0$ will be linearly independent, and together with the corresponding columns P^j will form a starting matrix for the desired problem. If $x = 0$ then $b = 0$, and

$$\begin{bmatrix} B \\ Q \end{bmatrix} = \begin{bmatrix} 1 \\ 0 \\ 0 \end{bmatrix}$$

is a starting matrix for the equivalent problem of

minimizing $\left| [0 \ P]\begin{bmatrix} t \\ x \end{bmatrix} - c \right|^2$

subject to $\begin{bmatrix} 1 & 0 \\ 0 & A \end{bmatrix}\begin{bmatrix} t \\ x \end{bmatrix} = \begin{bmatrix} 1 \\ 0 \end{bmatrix}$.

$$t, x \geq 0 \ .$$

This starting matrix is, however, degenerate, because $B = \begin{bmatrix} 1 \\ 0 \end{bmatrix}$ does not satisfy (A2).

6. PROOFS OF LEMMAS

Lemma 1

Suppose (A1) holds. Let (y^1, u^1) and (y^2, u^2) be solutions to (1), i.e.,

$$By^1 = b \qquad\qquad By^2 = b$$
$$\text{and}$$
$$B^T u^1 + Q^T Q y^1 = Q^T c \qquad B^T u^2 + Q^T Q y^2 = Q^T c \ .$$

Subtraction gives

$$B(y^1 - y^2) = 0 \tag{16}$$

and

$$B^T(u^1 - u^2) + Q^T Q(y^1 - y^2) = 0 \ . \tag{17}$$

Multiplying (17) by $(y^1 - y^2)^T$ and using the transpose of (16) gives

$$(y^1 - y^2)^T Q^T Q(y^1 - y^2) = 0 \ , \tag{18}$$

and (16) also implies that

$$(y^1 - y^2)^T B^T B(y^1 - y^2) = 0 \ ,$$

which added to (18) gives

$$(y^1 - y^2)^T [B^T Q^T] \begin{bmatrix} B \\ Q \end{bmatrix} (y^1 - y^2) = 0 \quad.$$

So

$$\begin{bmatrix} B \\ Q \end{bmatrix} (y^1 - y^2) = 0 \quad,$$

and (A1) implies that

$$y^1 = y^2$$

which, together with (17), implies that

$$B^T (u^1 - u^2) = 0 \quad.$$

Suppose, in addition to (A1), that (A2) holds. Then

$$u^1 = u^2 \quad.$$

Therefore, under assumptions (A1) and (A2), if (1) has a solution it is unique. We now show that (y,u) determined by the procedure of Section 3 is a solution to (1). Note that (15), (10), (12) and (13) imply sequentially that

$$By = BR^{-1}Wv + BR^{-1}\omega$$

$$= W^T Wv + W^T \omega$$

$$= S^T Sv + W^T \omega$$

$$= b - W^T \omega + W^T \omega \quad,$$

so

$$By = b \quad. \tag{19}$$

2.2 Lemma

Given $\varepsilon > 0$ and $\| h \| = 1$, we have that $(F(x + \varepsilon h) - F(x))/\varepsilon \geq F'(x,h) - K\varepsilon$.

Proof:

$$\frac{1}{\varepsilon} \max \{f(x + \varepsilon h, u): \quad u \in U\} - \frac{1}{\varepsilon} \max \{f(x,u): \quad u \in U\}$$

$$\geq \frac{1}{\varepsilon} \max \{f(x,u) + f'(x,u,h): \quad u \in U(x)\}$$

$$- K \, \varepsilon \, \| h \|^2 - F(x)/\varepsilon = \max \{f'(x,u,h): \quad u \in U(x)\}$$

$$- K\varepsilon \quad .$$

To proceed, another hypothesis on our max family is convenient. We shall assume if the index values u are close that jumps in $f'(y,\ldots,h)$ are bounded.

2.3 Lemma

Let x and y be arbitrary in E_ε and let $h = (y - x)/\| y - x \|$. Assume that for $\varepsilon > 0$, $\| x - y \| \geq \varepsilon$, $u_1 \in U(x)$ and $u_2 \in U(y)$ and $|F'_+(y,h)| \geq \sigma/2 > 0$; then

$$\frac{\left| f'(y,u_1,h) - f'(y,u_2,h) \right|}{\max \{|f'(y,u,h)|: \quad u \in U(y)\}} \leq r < 1 \quad .$$

Then there exists $\varepsilon_o \leq \varepsilon$ such that:

$$\frac{\left| F'_+(x,h) - F'_+(y,h) \right|}{|F'_+(y,h)|} \leq (1 + r)/2$$

whenever $\| x - y \| \leq \varepsilon_o$.

Proof: Take $\|x - y\| \leq \varepsilon$. Then

$$|F'_+(x,h) - F'_+(y,h)| = |\max \{f'(y,u,h) + f'(x,u,h)$$

$$- f'(y,u,h): \quad u \in U(x)\} - \max \{f'(y,u,h): \quad u \in U(y)\}|$$

$$\leq \max \{|f'(x,u,h) - f'(y,u,h)|: \quad u \in U(x)\}$$

$$+ |\max \{f'(y,u,h): \quad u \in U(x)\} - \max \{f'(y,u,h):$$

$$u \in U(y)\}| \leq ke_o + r|F'_+(y,h)| \quad .$$

Choose $\varepsilon_o \leq \dfrac{(1 - r)}{4K} \sigma$; then

$$\frac{|F'_+(x,h) - F'_+(y,h)|}{F'_+(y,h)} \leq \frac{1 + r}{2}$$

whenever $\|x - y\| \leq \varepsilon_o$.

2.4 *Lemma*

Assume the hypotheses of 2.3 with $x = P(y)$. Then $F(y) - F(P(y)) \geq \sigma/2\|y - P(y)\| (1 - q)$. By [18], if $|F'_+(x,h) - F'_+(y,h)| \leq q|F'_+(x,h)|$ then $(1 - q) |F'_+(y,y - P(y))| \leq |F(y) - F(P(y))|$. Since

$$q = \frac{1 + r}{2} \quad \text{and} \quad F'_+\left(y, \frac{y - P(y)}{\|y - P(y)\|}\right) \geq \sigma/2 \quad ,$$

the formula follows.

2.5 *Hypotheses*

We now collect some hypotheses.

(a) Given $x \in E_\varepsilon$, let $\sigma(x,\varepsilon) = \dfrac{f(x) - f(P(x))}{\varepsilon}$.

Since $f(P(x)) < f(x)$, $\sigma(x,\varepsilon) > 0$. We shall assume that: $\inf \{\sigma(x,\varepsilon): \quad x \in E_\varepsilon\} = \sigma > 0$.

(b) The hypothesis of 2.2.

(c) The hypothesis of 2.0.

2.6   Remark

Hypothesis (a) is proven in the finite dimensional case that follows in Section 3.

2.7   Theorem

As a consequence of the hypotheses of 2.5 the conditions A, B, and C are satisfied.

Proof:

[A] By 2.1, if $\varepsilon < \sigma/2K$, then $F'\left(y, \dfrac{P(y) - y}{\|P(y) - y\|}\right)$

$\leq -\sigma(x,\varepsilon) + \sigma/2 \leq -\sigma + \sigma/2 = -\sigma/2.$

Take $\phi(y) \in \partial f(y,u)$, then $[\phi(y),P(y) - y]$

$\leq F'(y,P(y) - y)$. Hence $[\phi(y),y - P(y)]$

$\geq \sigma/2\|y - P(y)\|$.

[B] By 2.0 F is Lipschitz continuous. For the lower bound, see 2.4.

[C] The existence of P follows by taking a minimizing sequence converging to $\mathrm{dist}(y,T(x,\varepsilon))$.

3. APPLICATION TO THE QUASIDIFFERENTIABLE FUNCTION OF PSHENICHNYI

3.0* Hypotheses

The following two hypotheses will be used in the sequel. Let S be an arbitrary subset of E_n.

---

*In this section the one-sided differential $f'_+(x,h)$ will be simply written as $f'(x,h)$.

[D]   f is locally Lipschitz on S and there exists $\hat{\varepsilon} > 0$
      such that if $0 < \varepsilon \leq \hat{\varepsilon}$ and x is in S then f achieves
      its minima on $B(x,\varepsilon)$ only on the boundary.

[E]   f is quasidifferentiable on S.   Thus, f is locally
      Lipschitz on S, $f'(x,.)$ exists for every x in S, and
      $f'(x,h) = \max \{[\phi,h]: \quad \phi \in \partial f(x)\}$ for every x in S
      and h in E_n.

3.1   Remarks

The concept of quasidifferentiability is used here as it is
in [13]; see also [15] and [16].   Clarke [17] has shown that
many "max" functions are quasidifferentiable.

For a quasidifferentiable function f it is true that each
$f'(x,.)$ is continuous.   Moreover, if 0 is not in $\partial f(x)$, it
follows that $f'(x,.)$ attains a unique minimum on the set of all
unit vectors.   To see this, note that

$$\min_{\|h\|=1} f'(x,h) = \min_{\|h\| \leq 1} \max \{[\phi,h]: \quad \phi \in \partial f(x)\}$$

$$= \max_{\|h\| \leq 1} \{\min [\phi,h]: \quad \phi \in \partial f(x)\}$$

$$= \max \{[\phi,-\phi/\|\phi\|]: \quad \phi \in \partial f(x)\}$$

$$= -\min \{\|\phi\|: \quad \phi \in \partial f(x)\} \quad ;$$

hence $f'(x,.)$ has its unique minimizer among unit vectors at
$-\phi_o/\|\phi_o\|$, where ϕ_o is the closest point to the origin in
$\partial f(x)$.

3.2   Definitions

Assume 3.0[D] and let $\hat{\varepsilon} > 0$ be as in 3.0[D].   Given $x \in S$
and ε in $[0,\hat{\varepsilon}]$, let $h(x,\varepsilon)$ be the set of *all* unit vectors h such

that $x + \varepsilon h$ minimizes f on $B(x,\varepsilon)$. Each vector in $h(x,\varepsilon)$ is called a direction of ε-*steepest descent*, while

$$\frac{f(x + \varepsilon h(x,\varepsilon)) - f(x)}{\varepsilon}$$

is called the *rate of ε-steepest descent*.

3.3 Lemma

Assume 3.0[E] and $x \in S$. Let $\{t_i\}$ be any positive sequence converging to 0, and let $h_i \in h(x,t_i)$ for each i. Let $\{t_k\}$ be a subsequence of $\{t_i\}$ such that $\{h_k\}$ converges to $h(0)$. Then

$$\lim_{k\to\infty} \frac{f(x + t_k h_k) - f(x)}{t_k} = \min \{f'(x,h): \; \|h\| = 1\}$$

$$= f'(x,h(0)) \quad.$$

Proof: By 3.1, $f'(x,.)$ has a unique minimizer h_o on the unit vectors. Then, $f(x + t_k h_k) - f(x) \leq f(x + t_k h_o) - f(x)$ for each k, and so

$$\lim_{k\to\infty} \sup \frac{f(x + t_k h_k) - f(x)}{t_k} \leq f'(x,h_o) \quad.$$

Also,

$$f'(x,h_o) \leq f'(x,h(0)) = \lim_{k\to\infty} \frac{f(x + t_k h(0)) - f(x)}{t_k}$$

$$= \lim_{k\to\infty} \inf \frac{f(x + t_k h_k) - f(x)}{t_k} + \lim_{k\to\infty} \frac{f(x + t_k h(0)) - f(x + t_k h_k)}{t_k}$$

$$= \lim_{k\to\infty} \inf \frac{f(x + t_k h_k) - f(x)}{t_k} \quad,$$

because of the Lipschitz condition on f. Therefore,

$$\lim_{k\to\infty} \frac{f(x + t_k h_k) - f(x)}{t_k} = f'(x,h_o) \quad ,$$

and moreover, $f'(x,h_o) = f'(x,h(0))$.

3.4 Remark

If 3.0[E] holds and if we put $h(x,0) = \{h_o\}$ (for each x in S), then the multifunction $t \to h(x,t)$ is, for each x in S, upper semicontinuous at 0.

3.5 Theorem

Assume 3.0[D] and 3.0[E]. For each x in S, the multifunction $h(x,.)$ is upper semicontinuous on $[0,\hat{\varepsilon})$.

Proof: By 3.4, $h(x,.)$ is upper semicontinuous at $t = 0$. Suppose $0 < t < \hat{\varepsilon}$. Let $\{\theta_i\}$ be a sequence of real numbers converging to 0 and let $\{h_i\}$ be a sequence of vectors such that each h_i is in $h(x, t + \theta_i)$ and $\{h_i\}$ converges to $\bar{h}$. Let $q_i = (t + \theta_i) h_i$ for each i. Then $\{q_i\}$ converges to $t\bar{h}$ and it must be shown that $\bar{h}$ is in $h(x,t)$. Two cases can be distinguished, accordingly as $\theta_i > 0$ for each i or $\theta_i < 0$ for each i.

Case (a). Suppose $\theta_i > 0$ for each i. Choose $x + p_i$ on the line segment which joins $x + th_i$ and $x + q_i$ such that $f(x + p_i) = f(x + th(x,t))$; this is possible because $f(x + th_i) \geq f(x + th(x,t)) > f(x + q_i)$. Hence, $|f(x + q_i) - f(x + th(x,t))| = |f(x + q_i) - f(x + p_i)| \leq L\|q_i - p_i\| \leq L\theta_i$, where L is a Lipschitz constant for f. Thus, $\lim_{i\to\infty} f(x + q_i) = f(x + t\bar{h}) = f(x + th(x,t))$ and so $\bar{h}$ is in $h(x,t)$.

Case (b). Suppose $\theta_i < 0$ for each i. Choose $h^{\sim}$ in $h(x,t)$ and choose $x + s_i$ on the line segment which joins $x + (t + \theta_i) h^{\sim}$

and $x + th^{\sim}$ such that $f(x + s_i) = f(x + q_i)$. This is possible, because $f(x + (t + \theta_i) h^{\sim}) \geq f(x + q_i) > f(x + th^{\sim})$. Much as before, one obtains $|f(x + q_i) - f(x + th^{\sim})| \leq L|\theta_i|$. Thus, $\lim_{i \to \infty} f(x + q_i) = f(x + t\bar{h}) = f(x + th^{\sim})$ and so $\bar{h}$ is again in $h(x,t)$.

3.6 *Miscellany*

The following information is from [17] and [19].

Let f be a locally Lipschitz function on E_n. In this setting, the Clarke generalized gradient $\partial f(x)$ is the convex hull of the limit points of all sequences $\{\nabla f(x + h_i)\}$ for which $\{h_i\} \to 0$. The ε-generalized gradient $\partial_\varepsilon f(x)$ is the convex hull of all limit points of $\{\nabla f(x_i)\}$ where $\{x_i\}$ converges to some point in $B(x,\varepsilon)$. The sets $\partial f(x)$ and $\partial_\varepsilon f(x)$ are convex and compact and the multifunctions $x \to \partial f(x)$ and $x \to \partial_\varepsilon f(x)$ are upper semicontinuous (in the Hausdorff metric).

Let B be a closed ball and let Z be the set of all *stationary* points x (i.e., $0 \in \partial f(x)$) in B. Given $\delta > 0$, put $B_\delta = \{x \in B: \|x - Z\| \geq \delta\}$. Then, by [19], there exist numbers $\varepsilon_1 > 0$ and $\sigma > 0$ such that, for each x in B_δ, $0 \notin \partial_{\varepsilon_1} f(x)$ and $\|\nabla_{\varepsilon_1} f(x)\| \geq \sigma$, where $\nabla_{\varepsilon_1} f(x)$ is the point in $\partial f_{\varepsilon_1}(x)$ closest to the origin. If one puts $h = \nabla_{\varepsilon_1} f(x)/\|\nabla_{\varepsilon_1} f(x)\|$ then $[h,\phi] \geq \sigma$ for all ϕ in $\partial_{\varepsilon_1} f(x)$ and $x \in B_\delta$; moreover, if $0 < \lambda \leq \varepsilon_1$ then $f(x + \lambda h) - f(x) \leq -\sigma\lambda$ (for each x in B). It follows that $\min \{f'(x,h): \|h\| = 1\} \leq -\sigma$ for all x in B_δ.

Finally, it should also be noted that if B_δ is chosen as above and if $S = B_\delta$ then 3.0[D] is automatically satisfied with $\hat{\varepsilon} = \delta$; this is an immediate consequence of the fact that any unconstrained local minimizer of f is a stationary point.

3.7 *Lemma*

Assume 3.0[E] with $S = B_\delta$ and let $M > 1$ be given. Then there exists $\varepsilon^{\sim} > 0$ such that $f'(x,h) \leq -\sigma/2$ whenever $x \in B_\delta$, $\varepsilon^{\sim}/M \leq \varepsilon \leq \varepsilon^{\sim}$, and $h \in h(x,\varepsilon)$.

Proof: Let $\varepsilon_2 = \min (\delta, \varepsilon_1)$. For each x in B_δ define $\varepsilon(x)$
$= \min \{\frac{1}{2} \varepsilon_2 \sup \{\varepsilon: f'(x,h) \leq -\sigma/2$ for $\varepsilon/M \leq \gamma \leq \varepsilon$ and h
$h(x,\gamma)\}\}$. Given x in B_δ, we know that $\varepsilon(x) > 0$, in view of
3.0[D], 3.5, and the inequality $f'(x,h(x,0)) \leq -\sigma$.

To complete the proof, we must show that

$$\varepsilon^\sim = \inf \{\varepsilon(x): \quad x \in B_\delta\} > 0 \quad . \tag{1}$$

Take a sequence $\{x_k\}$ in B_δ so that $\{\varepsilon(x_k)\}$ decreases monotonically to $\varepsilon^\sim$. Since B_δ is compact, we may require that $\{x_k\}$
converges to $\overline{x}$ in B_δ. Now define $\varepsilon^* = \min \{\frac{1}{2} \varepsilon_2, \sup \{\varepsilon:$
$f'(\overline{x},h) \leq -3\sigma/4$ for $0 \leq \gamma \leq \varepsilon$ and $h \in h(\overline{x},\gamma)\}\}$. As above,
$\varepsilon^* > 0$.

Let $\varepsilon \geq 0$ be given with $\varepsilon \leq \varepsilon^*$. Let $T_\varepsilon = \{y: f(y)$
$\leq f(\overline{x} + \varepsilon h(\overline{x},\varepsilon))\}$ and let P_ε denote the multifunction which
assigns to each y in B_δ the set of closest points in T_ε. There
exists k_o such that $\| x_k - \overline{x}\| < \varepsilon_2 - \varepsilon^*$ whenever $k \geq k_o$. For
$k \geq k_o$,

$$\| x_k - P_\varepsilon(x_k) \| \leq \| x_k - P_\varepsilon(\overline{x}) \|$$

$$\tag{2}$$

$$\leq \| x_k - \overline{x}\| + \|\overline{x} - P_\varepsilon(\overline{x}) \| < \varepsilon_2 \quad .$$

Define $\gamma(x_k,\varepsilon) = \| x_k - P_\varepsilon(x_k) \|$. Since $0 \leq \gamma(x_k,\varepsilon) < \delta$, we
know that f is minimized on $\beta(x_k,\gamma(x_k,\varepsilon))$ only at boundary points
and we have the equations

$$P_\varepsilon(x_k) = x_k + \gamma(x_k,\varepsilon) h(x_k,\gamma(x_k,\varepsilon)) \quad , \qquad k \geq k_o \quad ,$$

and $\tag{3}$

$$f(\overline{x} + \varepsilon h(\overline{x},\varepsilon)) = f(x_k + \gamma(x_k,\varepsilon) h(x_k,\gamma(x_k,\varepsilon))) \quad .$$

It is clear that, for $k \geq k_o$, each function $\gamma(x_k, \cdot)$ is nondecreasing on $[0, \varepsilon^*]$. At this point, we show that each such $\gamma(x_k, \cdot)$ is continuous on $[0, \varepsilon^*]$.

Thus, for $k \geq k_o$, suppose $0 < \varepsilon_o \leq \varepsilon^*$ and put $\alpha_k = \lim_{\varepsilon \to \varepsilon_o} \gamma(x_k, \varepsilon)$. It is clear that

$$\alpha_k \leq \gamma(x_k, \varepsilon_o) \quad . \tag{4}$$

Choose an increasing sequence $\{\varepsilon^j\}$ which converges to ε_o, and for each j, choose $h_j \in h(x_k, \gamma(x_k, \varepsilon^j))$; we may assume that $\{h_j\}$ converges to a unit vector h^*. From 3.7 and (3), we have $f(x_k + \alpha_k h^*) = \lim_{j \to \infty} f(x_k + \gamma(x_k, \varepsilon^j) \, h_j) = f(\overline{x} + \varepsilon_o h(\overline{x}, \varepsilon_o))$ and so $x_k + \alpha_k h^*$ is in T_{ε_o}. Hence $\gamma(x_k, \varepsilon_o) = \| x_k - P_{\varepsilon_o}(x_k) \| \leq \| \alpha_k h^* \| = \alpha_k$. In view of (4), it follows that $\gamma(x_k, \cdot)$ is left continuous at ε_o.

Let k remain fixed, suppose $0 \leq \varepsilon_o < \varepsilon^*$, and put $b_k = \lim_{\varepsilon \to \varepsilon_o} \gamma(x_k, \varepsilon)$. Again, it is clear that

$$b_k \geq \gamma(x_k, \varepsilon_o) \quad . \tag{5}$$

Fix $\eta > 0$. Since $h(x_k, \cdot)$ is upper semicontinuous at $\gamma(x_k, \varepsilon_o)$ there exists $\gamma > \gamma(x_k, \varepsilon_o)$, h_o^* in $h(x_k, \gamma(x_k, \varepsilon_o))$ and h_* in $h(x_k, \gamma)$ so $\gamma - \gamma(x_k, \varepsilon_o) < \eta$ and $\| h_o^* - h_* \| < \eta$. Set $x_k^* = x_k + \gamma h_*$. Then $f(x_k^*) < f(x_k + \gamma(x_k, \varepsilon_o) \, h(x_k, \gamma(x_k, \varepsilon_o))) = f(\overline{x} + \varepsilon_o h(\overline{x}, \varepsilon_o))$, by (3); hence, there exists $\varepsilon > \varepsilon_o$ so that $f(x_k^*) < f(\overline{x} + \varepsilon h(\overline{x}, \varepsilon))$. Therefore, $\gamma(x_k, \varepsilon) = \| x_k - P_\varepsilon(x_k) \| \leq \| x_k - x_k^* \| \leq \| x_k - (x_k + \gamma(x_k, \varepsilon_o) \, h_o^*) \| + \| x_k + \gamma(x_k, \varepsilon_o) \, h_o^* - (x_k + \gamma h_o^*) \| + \| x_k + \gamma h_o^* - (x_k + \gamma h_*) \| < \gamma(x_k, \varepsilon_o) + \eta + \gamma\eta$. Since $\eta > 0$ was otherwise arbitrary, it follows that $b_k \leq \gamma(x_k, \varepsilon_o)$ and, hence, from (5), that $\gamma(x_k, \cdot)$ is right continuous at ε_o.

Now, for each $k \geq k_o$ and ε in $[\varepsilon^*/2M, \varepsilon^*]$, we choose $v_k(\varepsilon)$ in the closed set $h(x_k, \gamma(x_k, \varepsilon))$ so as to maximize $f'(x_k, \cdot)$ over

$h(x_k, \gamma(x_k, \varepsilon))$. For each $k \geq k_o$ and ε in $[\varepsilon*/2M, \varepsilon*]$, we can, by 3.0[E], select $\phi_k(\varepsilon)$ in $\partial f(x_k)$ so that

$$f'(x_k, v_k(\varepsilon)) = [\phi_k(\varepsilon), v_k(\varepsilon)] \quad . \tag{6}$$

Assert now that an integer $k_1 \geq k_o$ exists so that

$$[\phi_k(\varepsilon), v_k(\varepsilon)] \leq -\frac{1}{2}\sigma \quad \text{for} \quad k \geq k_1 \quad \text{and}$$
$$\varepsilon*/2M \leq \varepsilon \leq \varepsilon* \quad . \tag{7}$$

If (7) were false, we could select an infinite subsequence $\{x_j\}$ of $\{x_k\}$ and a sequence $\{\varepsilon_j\}$ in the interval $[\varepsilon*/2M, \varepsilon*]$ so that $[\phi_j(\varepsilon_j), v_j(\varepsilon_o)] > -\sigma/2$ for each j, $\{\varepsilon_j\}$ converges to $\varepsilon^\#$, $\{v_j(\varepsilon_j)\}$ converges to $h^\#$, and $\{\phi_j(\varepsilon_j)\}$ converges to $\phi^\#$. Since ∂f is upper semicontinuous at $\bar{x}$, $\phi^\#$ is in $\partial f(\bar{x})$. By 3.0[E] and the definition of $\varepsilon*$, we get

$$-3\sigma/4 \geq f'(\bar{x}, h) \geq [\phi^\#, h] \quad , \quad \text{for every } h \text{ in } h(\bar{x}, \varepsilon^\#) \quad . \tag{8}$$

Next, we shall show that $h^\#$ is in $h(\bar{x}, \varepsilon^\#)$. If this were false, then there would be a unit vector h_1 so that

$$f(\bar{x} + \varepsilon^\# h_1) < f(\bar{x} + \varepsilon^\# h^\#) \quad . \tag{9}$$

For large j, the triangle inequality gives

$$\left| \; \|x_j - P_{\varepsilon_j}(x_j)\| - \|\bar{x} - P_{\varepsilon_j}(\bar{x})\| \; \right| \leq \|x_j - \bar{x}\| \quad ,$$

which amounts to $|\gamma(x_j, \varepsilon_j) - \varepsilon_j| \leq \|x_j - \bar{x}\|$. It follows that

$$\lim_{j \to \infty} \gamma(x_j, \varepsilon_j) = \varepsilon^\# \quad . \tag{10}$$

From (9), (10), and (3), we have for large j,

$$f(\overline{x} + \varepsilon_j h_1) < f(x_j + \gamma(x_j, \varepsilon_j) \ h(x_j, \gamma(x_j, \varepsilon_j)))$$

$$= f(\overline{x} + \varepsilon_j h(\overline{x}, \varepsilon_j)) \quad ; \tag{11}$$

But (11) contradicts the definition of $h(\overline{x}, \varepsilon_j)$ and so it must be true that $h^{\#}$ is in $h(\overline{x}, \varepsilon^{\#})$. Since $-\sigma/2 \leq \lim\limits_{j \to \infty} [\phi_j(\varepsilon_j), v_j(\varepsilon_j)]$ $= [\phi^{\#}, h^{\#}]$, the fact that $h^{\#}$ is in $h(\overline{x}, \varepsilon^{\#})$ leads to a contradiction of (8). Hence (7) is established.

From (6), (7), and the continuity of each $\gamma(x_k, .)$ we have, for $k \geq k_1$,

$$f'(x_k, h) \leq -\frac{1}{2} \sigma \quad \text{for} \quad \gamma(x_k, \varepsilon^*/2M) \leq \gamma \leq \gamma(x_k, \varepsilon^*) \quad \text{and}$$

$$h \in h(x_k, \gamma) \quad . \tag{12}$$

Arguing as we did for (10), we find $\lim\limits_{k \to \infty} \gamma(x_k, \varepsilon^*/2M) = \varepsilon^*/2M$ and $\lim\limits_{k \to \infty} \gamma(x_k, \varepsilon^*) = \varepsilon^*$. Hence there is an integer $k_2 \geq k_1$ such that, whenever $k \geq k_2$, we have $\gamma(x_k, \varepsilon^*/2M) \leq 2\varepsilon^*/3M$ and $\gamma(x_k, \varepsilon^*) \geq 2\varepsilon^*/3$. Hence (12) leads to $f'(x_k, h) \leq -\sigma/2$ whenever $2\varepsilon^*/3M \leq \gamma \leq 2\varepsilon^*/3$ and $h \in h(x_k, \gamma)$, provided $k \geq k_2$.

Therefore, it is true that $\varepsilon(x_k) \geq 2\varepsilon^*/3$ for $k \geq k_2$. It follows that (1) is true and that the proof is complete.

3.8 Remarks

Suppose that 1.0[A] is replaced by the weaker hypothesis:

1.0[A'] $[\phi(y), y - P(y)] \geq \Theta \, \| y - P(y) \|$

for y in D, provided $\| y - P(y) \| \geq \varepsilon/N$,

where $N \geq 2L/\mu$.

If this replacement is made, then the argument which yields Lemma 1.1 can be used to obtain a version of Lemma 1.1 with the following conclusion: "...there exists a smallest positive integer k* such that $\| x_{k*} - P(x_{k*}) \| < \varepsilon/N$; moreover, for $k = 0,\ldots,k*-1$, one has $\| x_k - P(x_k) \| \le \beta^k \| x_o - P(x_o) \|$, where $\beta = [1 - \mu^4/\alpha^4]^{1/2}$."

It is then easy to show that Theorem 1.3 will still be valid, with essentially the same proof, if 1.0[A] is replaced by the weaker 1.0[A'].

3.9 *Definitions*

Assume 3.0[E] with $S = B_\delta$ and let $\varepsilon > 0$. Given x in S, set $T(\varepsilon,x) = \{y: f(y) \le f(x + \varepsilon h(x,\varepsilon))\}$ and $D(\varepsilon,x) = \{y \in B_\delta: \| y - T(\varepsilon,x) \| \le \varepsilon\}$, and let $P = P_{\varepsilon,x}$ be the multifunction which associates with each y in $D(\varepsilon,x)$ the closest points to y in $T(\varepsilon,x)$. Define $\phi_{\varepsilon,x} = \phi$ by $\phi(y) = \{h/\| h \| : h \in \partial f(y)\}$.

3.10 *Theorem*

Let $\delta > 0$ and form the set B_δ as before. Assume 3.0[E] holds with $S = B_\delta$. There exists $\tilde{\varepsilon} > 0$ and there exist constants Θ, μ, L, α, and N such that for any x in B_δ and ε^* in $[\tilde{\varepsilon}/2,\tilde{\varepsilon}]$, with $T = T(\varepsilon^*,x)$, $D = D(\varepsilon^*,x)$, $\phi = \phi_{\varepsilon^*,x}$, and $P = P_{\varepsilon^*,x}$ as in 3.9, it is true that 1.0[A'], 1.0[B], and 1.0[C] hold.

Proof: Let L be the Lipschitz constant for f on B. Then put $\mu = \sigma$, $\Theta = \sigma/(2L)$, $\alpha = L/\Theta$, and $N = 2L/\sigma$. Let $M = 2N$ and choose $\tilde{\varepsilon}$ as given by Lemma 3.8 to correspond to M.

Now suppose $\tilde{\varepsilon}/2 \le \varepsilon^* \le \tilde{\varepsilon}$ and x is in B_δ. Since $\| y - T \| = \| y - P(y) \|$ for all y, it is obvious that 1.0[C] holds. If one sets $h = -\nabla_{\varepsilon^*}f(y)/\| \nabla_{\varepsilon^*}f(y) \|$, then by 3.6, $f(y) - f(P(y)) \ge f(y) - f(h + \| h - T \| h) \ge \sigma \| y - T \|$, for all y in D. Hence 1.0[B] is verified.

To see 1.0[A'], let y be in D with $\| y - T \| \ge \varepsilon^*/N$. Put $\varepsilon = \| y - T \| = \| y - P(y) \|$. Then $\varepsilon \ge \varepsilon^*/N = \tilde{\varepsilon}/M$ while $\varepsilon \le \varepsilon^* \le \tilde{\varepsilon}$. It follows from Lemma 3.7 that $f'(y,h(y,\varepsilon)) \le -\sigma/2$.

From 3.0[E] and from the equation $P(y) = y + \varepsilon h(y,\varepsilon)$, it follows that, for every ϕ in $\partial f(y)$, $[\phi, y - P(y)] = [\phi, -\varepsilon h(y,\varepsilon)] \geq \varepsilon\sigma/2$ $= \sigma/2 \|y - P(y)\| \geq (\sigma/2L)\|y - P(y)\| \|\phi\|$.

REFERENCES

[1] Cheney, E.W., and A.A. Goldstein, Newton's Method for Convex Programming and Chebyshev Approximation, *Numerische Mathematik*, 1 (1959), 253-268.

[2] Kelley, J.E., The Cutting Plane Method for Solving Convex Programs, *Journal of the Society for Industrial and Applied Mathematics*, 8, 4 (1960), 703-712.

[3] Shor, N.Z., *On the Structure of Algorithms for the Numerical Solution of Problems of Optimal Planning and Design*, Dissertation, Kiev, USSR, 1964 (in Russian).

[4] Shor, N.Z., Generalized Gradient Search, *Transactions of the 1st Winter School on Mathematical Programming*, held at Drogobich, Vol. 3, Moscow, 1969 (in Russian).

[5] Shor, N.Z., Utilization of the Operation of Space Dilation in the Minimization of Convex Functions, *Kibernetika*, 6, 1 (1970), 6-12; *Cybernetics*, 6, 1, 7-15.

[6] Shor, N.Z., Convergence Rate of the Gradient Descent Method with Dilation of the Space, *Kibernetika*, 6, 2 (1970), 80-85; *Cybernetics*, 6, 2, 102-108.

[7] Shor, N.Z., Generalized Gradient Methods for Non-Smooth Functions and Their Application to Mathematical Programming Problems, *Ekonomika i Matematicheskie Metody*, 12, 2 (1976), 337-356 (in Russian).

[8] Shor, N.Z., and N.G. Zhurbenko, A Minimization Method Using Space Dilation in the Direction of the Difference of Two Successive Gradients, *Kibernetika*, 4, 3 (1971), 51-59; *Cybernetics*, 7, 3, 450-459.

[9] Poljak, B.T., A General Method for Solving Extremal Problems, *Doklady, Akademii Nauk SSSR*, 174, 1 (1967), 33-36; *Soviet Math. Doklady*, 8 (1967), 593-597; Minimization of Unsmooth Functionals, *Zurnal Vycislitel'noi Matematiki i Matematiceskoi Fiziki*, 9 (1969), 509-521; *USSR Computational Mathematics and Mathematical Physics*, 9, 14-29.

[10] Bazenov, L.G., On Convergence Conditions of a Minimization Method of Almost-Differentiable Functions, *Kibernetika*, 8, 4 (1972), 71-72; *Cybernetics*, 8, 4, 607-609.

[11] Shor, N.Z., A Class of Almost-Differentiable Functions
      and a Minimization Method for Functions of This Class,
      Kibernetika, 8, 4 (1972), 65-70; *Cybernetics*, 8, 4,
      599-606.

[12] Nurminskii, E.A., Convergence Conditions for Nonlinear
      Programming Algorithms, *Kibernetika*, 8, 6 (1972),
      79-81; *Cybernetics*, 8, 6, 959-962.

[13] Pshenichnyi, B.N., *Necessary Conditions for an Extremum*,
      Nauka, Moscow, 1969 (English translation Marcel
      Dekker, New York, 1971).

[14] Clarke, F.H., A New Approach to Lagrange Multipliers,
      Mathematics of Operations Research, 1, 2 (1976),
      165-174.

[15] Mifflin, R., Semismooth and Semiconvex Functions in Con-
      strained Optimization, *SIAM Journal on Control and
      Optimization*, 15, 6 (1977), 959-972.

[16] Borwein, J.M., Fractional Programming Without Differen-
      tiability, *Mathematical Programming*, 11, 3 (1976),
      283-290.

[17] Clarke, F.H., Generalized Gradients and Applications,
      Transactions of the American Mathematical Society,
      205 (1975), 247-262.

[18] Goldstein, A.A., A Note on the Mean Value Theorem, *American
      Mathematical Monthly*, 79 (1972), 51-53.

[19] Goldstein, A.A., Optimization of Lipschitz Continuous
      Functions, *Mathematical Programming*, 13, 1 (1977),
      14-22.

NONSMOOTH OPTIMIZATION AND NONLINEAR PROGRAMMING

B. N. Pshenichnyi*

We first give an algorithm of the penalization type for
solving ordinary nonlinear programming problems in a "nondifferentiable optimization" context as in [1]. We investigate its
rate of convergence. Then we apply it for solving some more
specific problems such as finding a feasible point to a set
of equality and inequality constraints; and, finally, we give
some ideas which might lead to superlinearly convergent algorithms.

1. THE ALGORITHM

Let us consider an ordinary nonlinear programming problem

$$\left. \begin{array}{ll} \min f_o(x) & x \in R^n \\ \\ f_i(x) \le 0 & i \in I = \{1,2,\ldots,m\} \end{array} \right\} \tag{1}$$

in which we suppose the gradients $f_i'(x)$ to be Lipschitz continuous for $i = 0,1,\ldots,m$. For simplicity of notation, we suppose
also that there is a degenerate constraint $f_i(x) \equiv 0 \; \forall x$. We do
not require any Slater condition; in particular, the following
development will accept equality constraints $\ell(x) = 0$, simulated
by $f_i(x) = \ell(x)$, $f_{i+1}(x) = -\ell(x)$.

It would be possible to solve (1) by successive lineariza-
tions, i.e. by Newton's method, but the linearized problems

---

*This paper was written by C. Lemarechal from the tape recording
of the talk.

71

usually have no solution. This motivates the following algorithm, which has an NSO background.

Set

$$F(x) = \max\{f_i(x)/i \in I\} \quad \text{(note that } F(x) \geq 0\text{)} \qquad (2)$$

$$\phi_N(x) = f_o(x) + N F(x) \qquad \begin{array}{l} \text{for some positive} \\ \text{number N (}\phi_N \text{ is a} \\ \text{so-called exact} \\ \text{penalization)} \end{array} \qquad (3)$$

$$I_\delta(x) = \{i \in I/f_i(x) \geq F(x) - \delta\} \quad \text{for some } \delta > 0 \;. \qquad (4)$$

We will give a descent algorithm for minimizing $\phi_N(x)$, starting from some x_o.

Linearizing (1) about x, consider the following direction-finding problem in p:

$$\left.\begin{array}{ll} \min \; (f_o'(x),p) + \tfrac{1}{2}|p|^2 & p \in R^n \\[2em] (f_i'(x),p) + f_i(x) \leq 0 & i \in I_\delta(x) \;. \end{array}\right\} \qquad (5)$$

We suppose N and δ are chosen such that for any x in the level set $\{x/\phi_N(x) \leq \phi_N(x_o)\}$:

$$\text{Problem (5) is feasible} \qquad (6)$$

and

its Lagrange multipliers u_i satisfy

$$\sum_{i \in I_\delta(x)} u_i \leq N \quad . \tag{7}$$

Therefore, during the iterations of the algorithm, we can check (5) and (6): if (5) is infeasible, we decrease δ. If (7) does not hold, we increase N.

Let p(x) denote the solution of (5).

Theorem 1

p(x) = 0 if and only if x is feasible in (1) and it satisfies first order necessary optimality conditions.

It seems that, for computing p(x), it is more convenient to solve the dual of (5), namely

$$\left. \begin{array}{l} \min \tfrac{1}{2} \mid f_0'(x) + \displaystyle\sum_{i \in I_\delta(x)} u_i f_i'(x) \mid^2 - \displaystyle\sum_{i \in I_\delta(x)} u_i f_i(x) \\[2ex] u \geq 0 \end{array} \right\} \tag{8}$$

which, in addition, allows us to check (7).

Now the algorithm for minimizing $\phi_N(x)$ is iterative: knowing x_k, solve (5) (or (8)) to obtain $p(x_k) = p_k$. Then perform a step in the direction p_k:

$$x_{k+1} = x_k + \alpha_k p_k \qquad \alpha_k > 0 \tag{9}$$

The step size α_k gives a convergent algorithm provided it is chosen in the following way. Choose $\varepsilon \in\ ]\ 0,\ 1\ [$. Try $\alpha = 1$. If

$$\phi_N(x_k + \alpha p_k) \leq \phi_N(x_k) - \varepsilon\alpha \mid p_k \mid^2 , \tag{10}$$

then take this value. Otherwise replace α by a fixed fraction of itself until (10) is satisfied.

In other words, p_k is a direction from x_k, in which it is possible to decrease $\phi_N(x)$ by a significant amount, given by (10).

Theorem 2

$F(x_k) \rightarrow 0$. Every cluster point x^* of the sequence $\{x_k\}$ is feasible in (1) and satisfies the first order necessary optimality conditions. Furthermore, if (1) is a linear program, convergence is finite.

Because of the presence of δ, (5) might contain only a small number of constraints compared to those appearing in (1).

2. RATES OF CONVERGENCE

If no constraints are present in (1), the algorithm reduces to the ordinary gradient method. The rate of convergence is therefore usually linear. However, it becomes quadratic when the solution of (1) is a vertex (intersection of n constraints), i.e. when (1) looks like a linear program.

Let us investigate this point more precisely, because it will show how to modify the algorithm to obtain superlinear convergence.

Let x^* be a solution of (1). We suppose the standard second order sufficient optimality conditions are satisfied, namely

(i) $f_i'(x^*)$ $i \in I_0(x^*)$ are linearly independent;

(ii)   the (unique) Lagrange multipliers u^* are such that
$u_i^* > 0$, $i \in I_0(x^*)$;

(iii) $(p, L_{xx}''(x^*, u^*)p) > 0$ for any $p \neq 0$ such that
$(p, f_i'(x^*)) = 0$ $i \in I_0(x^*)$.

Concerning (i), a modification can be made to accept simulation of equality constraints (i.e., when $f_i(x) \leq 0$ and $-f_i(x) \leq 0$ are both present, one takes into account only one such constraint).

We can figure out the linear rate of convergence: let P be the projection mapping onto the subspace spanned by the active constraint gradients.

Lemma

The mapping $p(x)$ from R^n to R^n given by (5) is differentiable around x^* and its Jacobian is given by

$$p'(x^*) = - [P + (I - P)L''_{xx} (x^*,u^*)] \quad . \tag{11}$$

Now observe that $x_{k+1} = x_k + \alpha p(x_k)$ is just the standard process for solving $p(x) = 0$. It converges if the mapping $I + \alpha p'(x^*)$ has all its eigenvalues inside the unit circle. Then its rate of convergence is the largest modulus of all these eigenvalues.

It turns out that one can actually compute all these eigenvalues. Let $m = |I_o(x^*)|$ = number of active constraints at x^*. then $p'(x^*)$ has the following eigenvalues:

$\qquad$ m of them are equal to $- 1$;

$\qquad$ the $n - m$ remaining ones are equal to $- \gamma_i$
$\qquad$ where γ_i are the $n - m$ strictly positive
$\qquad$ eigenvalues of the symmetric matrix
$\qquad$ $(I - P)L''_{xx}(I - P)$.

Therefore the eigenvalues of the process (9) (with fixed α) are

$\qquad$ $1 - \alpha$ $\qquad\qquad$ m times

and

$\qquad$ $1 - \alpha\gamma_i$ $\qquad\qquad$ $n - m$ times.

These numbers are obviously smaller than 1. For ensuring convergence, they must be also greater than -1, which means that α must satisfy

$$\alpha < 2 \quad \text{and} \quad \alpha < \frac{2}{\gamma_i} \qquad i = 1,\ldots, n - m \quad .$$

The rate of convergence is then given by the smallest of these numbers. Hence, the Lagrange multipliers play a very important role for the rate of convergence. Roughly speaking, the larger m, the better the convergence. Ideally, when m = n, the choice $\alpha = 1$ makes all the eigenvalues zero, so that convergence is superlinear (Equation (9) reduces to Newton's method for solving a system of n equalities).

3. APPLICATIONS

Equations (5), (9) and (10) can be applied to solve a system of equalities and inequalities. In this case, $f_o(x) \equiv 0$ and (5) reduces to

$$\left. \begin{array}{l} \min \; |p|^2 \\[1.5em] (f_i'(x),p) + f_i(x) \le 0 \qquad I \in I_\delta(x) \end{array} \right\} \tag{12}$$

which is Newton's method.

Here, the assumptions (6) and (7) have to be modified, and we suppose now that there exists $\delta > 0$ such that

Problem (12) is feasible and
satisfies $|p(x)| \le C|F(x)|$. $\tag{13}$

This condition is satisfied for example if one supposes that the null-vector is never obtained by any *positive* combination of the active gradients: $\sum \lambda_i f_i'(x) \neq 0 \quad \forall \lambda_i \ge 0$.

Also the rule for choosing α is slightly different: we require

$$F(x_k + \alpha_k p_k) \le (1 - \alpha_k \varepsilon) \; F(x_k) \text{ for some } \varepsilon \in \;] \; 0, \; 1 \; [\quad . \tag{14}$$

Theorem 3

   (i) $x_k \to x^*$ and $F(x^*) \leq 0$

   (ii)   After a finite number of steps, $\alpha_k = 1$ satisfies (14)

   (iii)   After a finite number of steps, $F(x_{k+1}) \leq C\,F^2(x_k)$

   (iv) $|x_k - x^*| \leq C\,q^{2^k}$ with $q < 1$

   (v)   If the problem is linear, convergence is finite.

The algorithm can also be applied to minimize a max function of the form

$$f(x) = \max\{f_i(x)/i \in I\} \qquad \text{(I finite)} \quad .$$

Then expressions (1) reduce to

$$\left.\begin{aligned}
&\min \quad v \\[2mm]
&f_i(x) - v \leq 0 \qquad\qquad i \in I \quad .
\end{aligned}\right\} \tag{15}$$

It is then convenient not to consider (5) with $f_o = v$, but to modify it slightly and solve

$$\left.\begin{aligned}
&\min \quad \eta + \tfrac{1}{2}\,|p|^2 \qquad\qquad\qquad \eta \in R, \quad p \in R^n \\[2mm]
&(f_i'(x),p) + f_i(x) - \eta \leq 0 \qquad\qquad i \in I_\delta(x) \quad .
\end{aligned}\right\} \tag{16}$$

In this case, (6) and (7) are readily satisfied: (η,p) is feasible in (16) if η is large enough, and one can verify that the Lagrange multipliers sum up to 1. Hence, the choice of δ will depend only on computational convenience.

Theorem 2 applies. In particular, if the solution of (15) is a corner (i.e. $n + 1$ functions f_i are maximum at the solution), then convergence is quadratic. It would be interesting to generalize (16) to the case where the functions $f_i(x)$ are not explicitly known (in particular, when I is infinite).

4. IMPROVEMENT OF CONVERGENCE

Let us go back to (5). From (11), if $L_{xx}^{"}(x^*,u^*) = I$, then $p'(x^*) = -I$; all its eigenvalues are -1 and the choice of $\alpha_k = 1$ yields superlinear convergence. Therefore, any information about the optimal Lagrange multipliers might allow us to make a linear transformation on the variables which would generate a very small maximum eigenvalue for $(I + \alpha p')$.

For example, when x is near x^*, replacing (5) by

$$\min\ (f_o'(x),p) + \tfrac{1}{2}(p,L_{xx}^{"}(x^*,u^*)p) \qquad\qquad\Bigg\} \qquad (17)$$

$$(f_i'(x),p) + f_i(x) \le 0$$

would yield $p(x) = -(x - x^*) + o(|x - x^*|)$

and $u(x) = u^* + o(|x - x^*|)$.

To approximate (17), one could for example replace $L^{"}(x^*,u^*)$ by $L^{"}(x_k,u_{k-1})$ (u_{k-1} being the Lagrange multipliers of (17) with $x = x_{k-1}$).

REFERENCE

[1] Pshenichnyi, B.N., and Yu.M. Danilin, *Numerical Methods for Extremum Problems*, Nauka, Moscow, 1975 (in Russian); English translation forthcoming.

BUNDLE METHODS IN NONSMOOTH OPTIMIZATION

C. Lemarechal

This paper tries to synthesize what are called *conjugate subgradient methods*, and to extend them to a wider class of *bundle methods*. Also, we will show a connection with other methods primarily designed for solving ordinary mathematical programming problems. Our approach will be intuitive rather than algebraic: we will give not theorems, but ideas. Nothing essentially new will be said with respect to papers that have been published elsewhere.

We show that methods of conjugate gradients are perfectly justified as far as a local aspect is concerned, but that this local study is not enough for constructing efficient algorithms. We then try to replace the concept *local* by *finite neighborhood* and define the class of bundle methods. Finally we show that this class has a common background with many well-known methods.

Throughout the paper, $f(x)$ is a function defined on R^n, convex, and Lipschitz, the latter hypothesis being the most important. R^n is considered as a Hilbert space, i.e. we consider only the Euclidean norm. Also, we note that the dimension need not be finite; therefore we denote R^n by H.

1. LOCAL ASPECT

In this section, we have a point x, fixed in H, and we ask the question: how can we find a direction of descent, i.e. an element $d \in H$ such that the directional derivative

$$f'(x,d) = \lim_{t \downarrow 0} \frac{f(x + td) - f(x)}{t} \tag{1}$$

is strictly negative.

We follow Clarke's analysis [1]; as a Lipschitz function, f has a gradient almost everywhere in H. It is therefore possible to construct sequences $\{x_i\}$ such that $\nabla f(x_i)$ exists and $x_i \rightarrow x$. The corresponding sequences $\{\Delta f(x_i)\}$ are bounded and have (weak) cluster points. Define the set of all such cluster points:

$$M(x) = \{g \mid g = \lim \nabla f(x_i), \ x_i \rightarrow x, \ \nabla f(x_i) \text{ exists}\} \ . \quad (2)$$

Then there exists between (1) and (2) the following basic relation:

$$f'(x,d) = \sup \{(d,g) \mid g \in M(x)\} \ . \quad (3)$$

From this, several observations follow:

(a) The property that d is a descent direction implies that -d makes an acute angle with every g in M(x). The set of descent directions is the (open) polar cone of the convex cone generated by M(x).

(b) M(x) represents exactly the behavior of f in the neighborhood of x. Knowing a descent direction implies a *complete study* of f around x. It is not a trivial problem in general, unless f is differentiable at x (M(x) is the singleton $\nabla f(x)$), or when f is made up of a *finite* number of *known differentiable* functions f_i which meet at x (then M(x) is made up of the gradients $\nabla f_i(x)$).

(c) Any descent direction defines a hyperplane separating the convex sets $\{0\}$ and $\{\text{conv } M(x)\}$. Therefore, x is optimal iff there is no such hyperplane, i.e. $0 \in \text{conv } \{M(x)\}$. Accordingly, it is interesting to consider not M(x) alone, but its convex hull $\partial f(x) = \text{conv } M(x)$ (see also (a) above) which is the ordinary subdifferential [11].

(d) The *best* descent direction is defined as solving the problem

$$\min_{d} f'(x,d) \iff \min_{d} \max \{(g,d) \mid g \in \partial f(x)\} \ . \quad (4)$$

Of course, the directional derivative being in essence a positively homogeneous function of d, it is necessary to normalize d. Then, *when the Euclidean norm is chosen*, it is possible to show, through some tedious calculations, that the optimal d is opposite to

$$Nr \ \partial f(x) = Proj \ 0/\partial f(x) \ , \tag{5}$$

i.e. the point of minimal Euclidean norm in $\partial f(x)$. (We note here that, in the differentiable case, the optimal d in the ℓ_1 sense would be a vector of the canonical basis; in this framework, the *steepest descent* method would be Gauss-Seidel!)

(e) Of course, the probability for M(x) not to be a singleton is zero. However, x might be so close to a point of nondifferentiability that it is impossible to find a numerically nonzero step size in the direction $-\nabla f(x)$. We are in fact interested in constructing directions that are numerically usable. From this viewpoint, there is no difference between a nondifferentiable function and a stiff function: they differ only on a set of measure 0. Accordingly, our development will be valid also for minimizing ordinary but ill-conditioned functions. ∥

Now we give the basic ideas for constructing a descent direction or, equivalently, for constructing M(x). Suppose we know k points in M(x):

$$\{g_1, \ldots, g_k\} \subset M(x)$$

for some integer k. This is initialized by computing g_1 directly. In view of (e) above, one generally has $g_1 = \nabla f(x)$. Knowledge of one point in M(x) is really the minimal requirement for using a method based on gradients.

The question is: knowing this partial information about M(x), is it possible to deduce a descent direction easily? If not, how can we determine some $g_{k+1} \in M(x)$ so as to improve the current approximation?

Since $f'(x,d) \geq \max \{(d,g_i)|i = 1,...,k\}$, we choose some d_k satisfying

$$(d_k,g_i) < 0 \qquad i = 1,...,k \; . \qquad (6)$$

We hope that d_k is a descent direction; so, to check it, we tabulate the function $f(x + td_k)$ for $t \downarrow 0$. Then,

- either we find $t > 0$ such that $f(x + td_k) < f(x)$ and we are done,
- or $f(x + td_k) \geq f(x)$ for any t generated by this line search.

This is the only interesting case here. By convexity, for any $t > 0$ and for any $g \in M(x + td_k)$

$$f(x + td_k) \geq f(x) \geq f(x + td_k) + (g,x - x - td_k) \; .$$

Passing to the limit and denoting by g_{k+1} any cluster point of g, $g_{k+1} \in M(x)$ by definition. Furthermore one has

$$(g_{k+1},d_k) \geq 0 \; . \qquad (7)$$

Comparing (6) and (7), we see that, increasing k by 1 and computing a new d satsifying (6), we will certainly get a different direction.

Note that property (7) comes directly from convexity of f, which therefore seems essential. In fact it can be weakened to the so-called *weak upper semismoothness* [8] which, roughly speaking, implies: if the differential quotient $[f(x + td) - f(x)]/t$ goes to a positive limit, then the corresponding slope (g,d) (where $g \in M(x + td)$) goes also to a positive limit. ||

Now recall that we are trying to construct M(x). In view of (6) and (7), in order for g_{k+1} to be *as good as possible*, d_k

should make the numbers (d_k, g_i) *as negative as possible*. This justifies a min-max strategy, which consists in computing d_k as solving

$$\min_{d} \max \{(d, g_i) \mid i = 1, \ldots, k\} \quad . \tag{8}$$

Again it is necessary to bound d; again, when using the Euclidean norm, (8) turns out to have the solution $d_k = -Nr\{g_1, \ldots, g_k\}$. Note that this gives $d_1 = -g_1$ for k = 1. It is then just technical to prove that, if x is not optimal, the above process is finite, thanks to (7),(8), and the boundedness of $\{g_k\}$. When x is optimal $d_k \to 0$ (strongly), and, since $-d_k \in \partial f(x)$, this provides a stopping test. Note that when M(x) is finite, the process is finite anyway.

To conclude this section we state that, knowing a convex set G included in $\partial f(x)$, *the best we can do* is to compute its vector of minimal length.

-   If $G = \partial f(x)$ we then get the steepest descent direction.

-   If G is a sufficient approximation of $\partial f(x)$, we get some descent direction.

-   If G is too poor an approximation we can generate a new point in M(x) and improve G by an infinite line-search. Repeating the process, it is then possible to find a descent direction, if any.

2. NUMERICAL ASPECT: ENLARGEMENT OF THE SUBDIFFERENTIAL

In the previous development, several questions remain open.

(a) Keep in mind Section 1(e). Strictly speaking, the process for constructing M(x) is useless since it is probably a singleton.

(b) Suppose we try to minimize f by the following algorithm:

-   x_k being given, first compute a descent direction d_k by the process of Section 1.

- Then move along d_k, for example with an optimal
step size.

This, at best, simulates the steepest descent method, which is known to be slow, and may converge to a nonoptimal point when f is really nondifferentiable. In other words, this algorithm would converge very slowly to a nonoptimal point!

(c) For computing a descent direction--more specifically, for generating new points in M(x)--we are supposed to perform infinite line-searches along each trial direction, with $t \rightarrow 0$. This is forbidden. ‖

It appears that these phenomena come from the same imperfection: M(x) is too small, containing only limits of gradients. Suppose, on the contrary, that we replace in (2) the concept "$x_i \rightarrow x$" by "x_i close enough to x". More precisely, for $\varepsilon > 0$ define some neighborhood $V_\varepsilon(x)$ (for example the ball of radius ε). Then enlarge M(x) as follows

$$M(x) \subset M_\varepsilon(x) = \{g | g = \lim \nabla f(x_i), x_i \rightarrow y, y \in V_\varepsilon(x)\} \quad , \quad (9)$$

which directly follows Goldstein's analysis [3]. This new definition eliminates the above-mentioned phenomena:

(a') $M_\varepsilon(x)$ is never a singleton--unless f is linear, at
least in $V_\varepsilon(x)$ (not an interesting case).

(b') If a direction d satsifies $(d,g) < 0 \; \forall \; g \in M_\varepsilon(x)$, it can be seen by integration that $f(x + td)$ is a decreasing function of t as long as $x + td \in V_\varepsilon(x)$. A line-search along d will get us out of $V_\varepsilon(x_n)$, and, from compactness, we will converge in a finite number of steps to some x_N such that $V_\varepsilon(x_N)$ contains the minimum of f.

(c') Constructing $M_\varepsilon(x)$ is easier than constructing M(x) in the sense that we can stop the line-search along a trial direction d_k as soon as $x + td_k \in V_\varepsilon(x)$, i.e. for some finite $t > 0$. ‖

Several enlargements of M(x) are possible. One of them, coming from convex analysis, is particularly interesting, despite

the fact that it is difficult to define the corresponding $V_\varepsilon(x)$.
We define directly the convex set

$$\partial_\varepsilon f(x) = \{g \,|\, \forall\, y \in H,\ f(y) \geq f(x) + (g,y - x) - \varepsilon\} \ . \quad (10)$$

(a") This set contains $\partial f(x)$. Also $\partial_\varepsilon f(x) = \partial f(x)$ only in
very special situations. Moreover, it is a closed, convex, and
(weakly) compact set (because f is Lipschitz).

(b") There exists the following basic relation [11, p.220]:

$$\inf_{t>0} \frac{f(x + td) - f(x) + \varepsilon}{t} = \sup\{(d,g) \,|\, g \in \partial_\varepsilon f(x)\} \ . \quad (11)$$

which directly extends (3). It follows that $0 \in \partial_\varepsilon f(x) \Longleftrightarrow$ x minimizes f within ε. Also, if d is such that $(d,g) < 0\ \forall\, g \in \partial_\varepsilon f(x)$,
then (and only then) it is possible to find t > 0 such that
$f(x + td) < f(x) - \varepsilon$.

(c") Let x and y be two different points in H. Let $g \in \partial f(y)$
and $\varepsilon \geq 0$. Then $g \in \partial_\varepsilon f(x)$ iff

$$f(y) \geq f(x) + (g,y - x) - \varepsilon \ . \quad (12)$$

This formula can be looked at from different angles:

(i) x, y, $g \in \partial f(y)$ are given. Then $g \in \partial_\varepsilon f(x)$ for any
$\varepsilon \geq f(x) + (g,\ y - x) - f(y)$ (a known positive number).

(ii) y, $g \in \partial f(y)$, $\varepsilon \geq 0$ are given. Then $g \in \partial_\varepsilon f(x)$ for
any x such that $f(x) - (g,x) \leq f(y) - (g,y) + \varepsilon$, i.e. for any x
close enough to y.

(iii) x and $\varepsilon \geq 0$ are given. For any y, any $g \in \partial f(y)$ is
also in $\partial_\varepsilon f(x)$ provided $f(y) + (g,x - y) \geq f(x) - \varepsilon$. By continuity this is again true whenever y is close enough to x (g is
bounded since f is Lipschitz). Observe that the left-hand side
of this inequality is the value at x of the approximation of f
linearized at y.

In particular, when y is the current point x + td of some line-search, $g \in \partial f(x + td)$ belongs also to $\partial_\varepsilon f(x)$ when $f(x + td) - t(g,d) \geq f(x) - \varepsilon$, and this is eventually true provided $t \to 0$. ‖

Thus, the introduction of $\partial_\varepsilon f(x)$ does not explicitly define $V_\varepsilon(x)$, but rather makes precise the concept *close enough to* in terms of objective value units. This is the really good feature of this set: it makes us able to compare movements Δx in H with the common measure of movements Δf in R. Of course, (12) is very useful since we can only generate points g of the form $\nabla f(y)$, and they must be *transported* into sets $\partial_\varepsilon f(x)$.

Note that $-Nr\ \partial f(x)$ has a good geometrical interpretation: it is the steepest descent direction. Here, $-Nr\ \partial_\varepsilon f(x)$ has no such simple interpretation. We can only say that there exists $\eta(\varepsilon) > 0$ such that $-Nr\ \partial_\varepsilon f(x)$ points towards the projection of x onto the level line $f(x) - \varepsilon - \eta(\varepsilon)$ (if such a level line exists, i.e. if $f(x) > \min f + \varepsilon$). ‖

As the first application of this enlargement, we can adapt the algorithm of Section 1 to construct $\partial_\varepsilon f(x)$, or equivalently to determine an ε-*descent direction*, i.e. a direction d such that $\inf \{f(x + td)|t > 0\} < f(x) - \varepsilon$. Let x be fixed, and choose $\varepsilon > 0$. Suppose k points $g_1, \ldots, g_k$ are already known in $\partial_\varepsilon f(x)$. Determine d_k such that $(d_k, g_i) < 0$ i = 1,...,k. Again it is interesting to choose $d_k = -Nr \{g_1, \ldots, g_k\}$. Make a line-search along d_k. If we can decrease by ε, we are done. Therefore, suppose $f(x + td_k) \geq f(x) - \varepsilon$ for any t generated by the line-search. Two cases may occur:

(j) $f(x + td_k) \geq f(x)\ \forall\ t$. Then we are exactly in the situation described in Section 1. $(g,d_k) \geq 0\ \forall\ t > 0$, $\forall\ g \in \partial f(x + td_k)$, and we can stop the line-search as soon as $t \leq [f(x + td_k) - f(x) + \varepsilon]/(g,d_k)$ which eventually occurs (f is Lipschitz: (g,d_k) cannot go to $+\infty$).

(jj) Slightly more complicated is the case where some t_L is produced during the course of the line-search, such that:

$$f(x) > f(x + t_L d_k) \geq f(x) - \varepsilon \quad .$$

Then it might be impossible to produce a positive t such that
any $g \in \partial f(x + td_k)$ simultaneously satisfies $g \in \partial_\varepsilon f(x)$ and
$(g, d_k) \geq 0$.

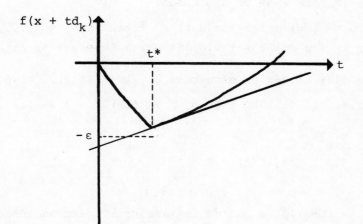

$f(x + td_k)$

t^*

t

$-\varepsilon$

This sketch is a counter-example: there is a minimizing $t^* > 0$
along d_k. The set L of step sizes generating ε-subgradients at
x is $[0, t^*[$. The set R of step sizes generating gradients satisfying (7) is $]t^*, +\infty[$ and $L \cap R = \phi$. In fact g_{k+1} should be a
particular subgradient at the *optimal* t^*.

In that situation, the gimmick consists in computing g_{k+1}
as a convex combination of $g_L \in \partial f(x + t_L d_k)$, $t_L \in L$, and $g_R \in$
$\partial f(x + t_R d_k)$, $t_R \in R$. We choose this combination such that
$(g_{k+1}, d_k) \simeq 0$; and $g_{k+1} \in \partial_\varepsilon f(x)$ if $t_R - t_L$ is small enough. ‖

This is the ε-descent method given in [4]. It has a curious
variant, in which we just neglect the test $f(x + td_k) < f(x) - \varepsilon$,
and we never move from x. Let us give its schematic description:
fix $x \in H$. Let $g_1 \in \partial f(x)$. Set $k = 1$.

- Compute $d_k = -Nr \{g_1, \ldots, g_k\}$.

- Minimize $f(x + td_k)$ for $t \geq 0$ and get an optimal $t_k \geq 0$.

- Compute $g_{k+1} \in \partial f(x + t_k d_k)$ such that $(g_{k+1}, d_k) = 0$.

Set $k = k + 1$ and go to 1. ‖

Of course, the second and third steps are only schematic. One must simulate them by the development (j), (jj) above. The proof of convergence is fairly illustrative of what is done generally in this kind of algorithm:

Set $\alpha_k = f(x) - f(x + t_k d_k)$, $\varepsilon_k = \max \{\alpha_i | i = 1,\ldots,k\}$ and denote by x_k the point $x + t_i d_i$ at which this max is attained.

From (12) it can be seen that $g_{i+1} \in \partial_{\alpha_i} f(x)$. Also $\alpha_i \leq \varepsilon_k$ $i = 1,\ldots,k$. It follows that $g_i \in \partial_{\varepsilon_k} f(x)$ $i = 1,\ldots,k+1$; therefore

$$-d_{k+1} \in \partial_{\varepsilon_k} f(x) \quad .$$

Now pass to the limit: as an increasing bounded sequence $\varepsilon_k \to \varepsilon^* = f(x) - \lim f(x_k)$. As in Section 1, $d_{k+1} \to 0$. There is a general result of uppersemicontinutiy of the subdifferential, which says that in this situation, $0 \in \partial_{\varepsilon^*} f(x)$. Hence, from (11): $f(x) \leq \min f + \varepsilon^*$, which means

$$\lim f(x_k) \leq \min f \quad . \quad ||$$

3. CONSTRUCTING DESCENT ALGORITHMS: BUNDLE METHODS

So far, we have only considered f near a fixed x, strictly locally in Section 1, in a fixed neighborhood in Section 2. Now suppose we have performed several steps of some descent method. A certain number of points have been generated, at which the value of f has been computed together with some subgradient. We symbolize this information by the *bundle* $x_1,\ldots,x_k$; $f_1,\ldots,f_k$; $g_1,\ldots,g_k$, where $f_i = f(x_i)$ and $g_i \in \partial f(x_i)$. We denote $G_k = \{g_1,\ldots,g_k\}$.

This labeling is therefore not that of iterations. In fact we can store what we want, from just $\{x_k, f_k, g_k\}$ to all the information generated during all the line-searches from the beginning of the algorithm. This is purely a matter of core requirement.

By (14) and (9) we have

$$B^T u + Q^T Qy = B^T(b - v) + (R^T R - B^T B)y \ .$$

Now (19), (15), (10) and (11) imply sequentially that

$$B^T u + Q^T Qy = B^T b - B^T v + R^T Ry - B^T b$$

$$= -B^T v + R^T(Wv + \omega)$$

$$= -B^T v + B^T v + Q^T c \ ,$$

so (y,u) solves (1).

Lemma 2

Since $\frac{1}{2}|Qy - c|^2$ is convex in y and By is linear in y, the conditions given by (1) are well known to be both necessary and sufficient for optimality in the problem of minimizing $\frac{1}{2}|Qy - c|^2$ subject to By = b. Multiplying on the left (1a) by u^T and (1b) by y^T, and differencing the resulting equations, give

$$u^T By - y^T B^T u - y^T Q^T Qy = u^T b - y^T Q^T c$$

which, by scalar transposition, is equivalent to

$$y^T Q^T Qy = -b^T u + c^T Qy$$

which is equivalent to (2).

Lemma 3

Combining the definition of x and (1) gives

$$Ax = By = b \ ,$$

$$Px = Qy \tag{20}$$

and

$$B^T u + Q^T (Px - c) = B^T u + Q^T (Qy - c) = 0 \quad . \tag{21}$$

Also, $y \geq 0$ implies $x \geq 0$. Combining (20), (21) and (3) implies

$$A^T_j u + P^T_j (Px - c) \geq 0 \qquad \text{for each } j = 1,2,\ldots,n$$

with strict inequality only if $x_j = 0$.

Thus, x and u satisfy the optimality conditions.

Lemma 4

Suppose, for purposes of a proof by contradiction, that

$$\begin{bmatrix} B & A^\ell \\ Q & P^\ell \end{bmatrix} \begin{bmatrix} \lambda \\ \lambda_\ell \end{bmatrix} = 0 \tag{22}$$

for some nonzero vector $(\lambda, \lambda_\ell)^T$. Note that

$$\lambda_\ell \neq 0 \quad , \tag{23}$$

because, by assumption, $\begin{bmatrix} B \\ Q \end{bmatrix}$ has full column rank. Multiplying (22) on the left by $(u^T, y^T Q^T - c^T)$ gives

$$\left(u^T B + (y^T Q^T - c^T) Q \right) \lambda + \left(u^T A^\ell + (y^T Q^T - c^T) P^\ell \right) \lambda_\ell = 0 \quad .$$

But this is a contradiction, because the first term is zero by the transpose of (1b) and the second term is nonzero by (23) and the transpose of (4).

Lemma 5

By the remark following Lemma 4, Lemma 1 applied to (1)$^+$ implies that (1)$^+$ has a solution (y^+, y_ℓ^+, u^+). Since

$$[B \ A^{\ell}] \begin{bmatrix} y \\ 0 \end{bmatrix} = b \quad ,$$

Lemma 2 applied to (1)$^+$ implies that

$$\left| [Q \ P^{\ell}] \begin{bmatrix} y^+ \\ y_{\ell}^+ \end{bmatrix} - c \right|^2 \leq \left| [Q \ P^{\ell}] \begin{bmatrix} y \\ 0 \end{bmatrix} - c \right|^2 = \left| Qy - c \right|^2 \quad . \tag{24}$$

By (2) of Lemma 2 applied to (1)$^+$ and (1), we have

$$\left| [Q \ P^{\ell}] \begin{bmatrix} y^+ \\ y_{\ell}^+ \end{bmatrix} - c \right|^2 - \left| Qy - c \right|^2 =$$

$$= -b^T u^+ - c^T (Qy^+ + P^{\ell} y_{\ell}^+ - c) + b^T u + c^T (Qy - c)$$

$$= -b^T u^+ - c^T Qy^+ - c^T P^{\ell} y_{\ell}^+ + b^T u + c^T Qy \quad . \tag{25}$$

Multiplying the transposes of (1a) and (1b) on the right by u^+ and y^+, respectively, and (1a)$^+$, (1b)$^+$ and (1c)$^+$ on the left by $-u^T$, $-y^T$ and y_{ℓ}^+, respectively, and then adding the resulting equations gives

$$y^T B u^+ + u^T B y^+ + y^T Q^T Q y^+ - u^T B y^+ - u^T A y_{\ell}^+ - y^T B^T u^+ -$$

$$- y^T Q^T Q y^+ - y^T Q^T P^{\ell} y_{\ell}^+ = b^T u^+ + c^T Q y^+ - u^T b - y^T Q^T c$$

which, after cancellation and rearrangement, is equivalent to

$$0 = u^T A^{\ell} y_{\ell}^+ + y^T Q^T P^{\ell} y_{\ell}^+ + b^T u^+ + c^T Q y^+ - u^T b - y^T Q^T c \quad .$$

Adding this to (25) and simplifying gives

$$\left| [Q \ P^{\ell}] \begin{bmatrix} y^+ \\ y_{\ell}^+ \end{bmatrix} - c \right|^2 - \left| Qy - c \right|^2 = (u^T A^{\ell} + y^T Q^T P^{\ell} - c^T P^{\ell}) \ y_{\ell}^+ \tag{26}$$

which, by transposition, is equivalent to the equality in (5). Now (24), (26) and (4) imply that $y_\ell^+ \geq 0$. Suppose $y_\ell^+ = 0$. Then, by $(1a)^+$ and $(1b)^+$, (y^+, u^+) solves (1). But assumptions (A1) and (A2) imply, by Lemma 1, that $(y^+, u^+) = (y, u)$. Then, since we suppose $y_\ell^+ = 0$, (4) and $(1c)^+$ are contradictory. Therefore, $y_\ell^+ > 0$, which together with (26) and (4) gives the desired inequality in (5) and completes the proof.

Lemma 6

Since $y > 0$ and $y_\ell^+ > 0$, $\bar{\lambda}$ is well defined by

$$\bar{\lambda} = \min\left\{1, \min\left[y_j / (y_j - y_j^+) : y_j - y_j^+ > 0, \; j \in J\right]\right\}$$

and we have $\bar{\lambda} > 0$, $z_\ell = \bar{\lambda} y_\ell^+ > 0$ and $z_j \geq 0$ for all $j \in J$. Moreover, z has at least one zero component if and only if $y^+ \ngtr 0$. The definition of z combined with (1a) and $(1a)^+$ implies (6) and, combined with the convexity of quadratic functions having positive semidefinite Hessian matrices, implies that

$$\left| [Q \; P^\ell] z - c \right|^2 \leq \bar{\lambda} \left| [Q \; P^\ell] \begin{bmatrix} y^+ \\ y_\ell^+ \end{bmatrix} - c \right|^2 + (1 - \bar{\lambda}) \left| Qy - c \right|^2 .$$
(27)

Finally, (7) follows from (27) and (5).

Lemma 7

By construction at Step 3, $\bar{y}$ satisfies

$$\bar{y} > 0 \quad \text{and} \quad \begin{bmatrix} B^- \\ Q^- \end{bmatrix} \bar{y} = \begin{bmatrix} B \\ Q \end{bmatrix} z .$$
(28)

Also, $J^- \subset J$, so $\begin{bmatrix} B^- \\ Q^- \end{bmatrix}$ has full column rank, because $\begin{bmatrix} B \\ Q \end{bmatrix}$ has full column rank. By (28) and (H) we have

$$B^- \bar{y} = b ,$$
(29)

so, by the remark following Lemma 2, y^- is well defined and

$$B^- y^- = b .$$ (30)

Therefore, by Lemma 2 and (28),

$$|Q^- y^- - c|^2 \leqq |Q^- \bar{y} - c|^2 = |Qz - c|^2 .$$ (31)

If $y^- > 0$, then (8) follows from (31) and the hypothesis that

$$|Qz - c|^2 < |Q^\circ y^\circ - c|^2 .$$ (32)

Suppose $y^- \not= 0$. Then, because $\bar{y} > 0$, at the next execution of Step 3, $\bar{\lambda}$ and z^- are well defined and we have

$$\bar{\lambda} > 0 ,$$

$$z^- = \bar{\lambda} y^- + (1 - \bar{\lambda}) \bar{y} \geqq 0 ,$$

and

$$z^-_k = 0 \quad \text{for some } k .$$

Also, by (29) and (30), we have

$$B^- z^- = b$$ (33)

and, by objective convexity, (31) and (32), we have

$$|Q^- z^- - c|^2 \leqq |Q^- \bar{y} - c|^2 = |Qz - c|^2 < |Q^\circ y^\circ - c|^2 .$$ (34)

If $z^-_{\ell^\circ} = 0$ then, since $J^- \subset J^\circ \cup \{\ell^\circ\}$, (33) and Lemma 2 imply that

$$|Q^\circ y^\circ - c|^2 \leqq |Q^- z^- - c|^2 ,$$

which contradicts (34). Therefore, $z^-_{\ell^\circ} > 0$ and the proof is complete.

REFERENCES

[1] Gill, P.E., G.H. Golub, W. Murray, and M.A. Saunders, Methods for Modifying Matrix Factorizations, *Mathematics of Computation*, 28, 126 (1974), 505-535.

[2] Golub, G.H., and M.A. Saunders, Linear Least Squares and Quadratic Programming, in J. Abadie, ed., *Integer and Nonlinear Programming*, North-Holland, Amsterdam, 1970, ch. 10.

[3] Lawson, C.L., and R.J. Hanson, *Solving Least Squares Problems*, Prentice-Hall, Englewood Cliffs, N.J., 1974.

[4] Lemarechal, C., Combining Kelley's and Conjugate Gradient Methods, *Abstracts, 9th International Symposium on Mathematical Programming*, Budapest, 1976.

[5] Stoer, J., On the Numerical Solution of Constrained Least-Squares Problems, *SIAM J. Numerical Analysis*, 8, 2 (1971), 382-411.

[6] Wolfe, P., Finding the Nearest Point in a Polytope, *Mathematical Programming*, 11, 2 (1976), 128-149.

SUFFICIENT MINIMIZATION OF PIECEWISE-LINEAR UNIVARIATE FUNCTIONS*

P. Wolfe

PRELIMINARIES

Minimization of a function of a single variable is a fundamental subroutine in most procedures for the minimization of
functions of many variables. We now know of important classes
of large-scale linear programming problems, having astronomically
many variables, which can be recast as problems of minimizing
convex, nonlinear but piecewise-linear, functions of reasonable
numbers of variables. The "method of conjugate subgradients"
is a procedure for solving the latter kind of problem, requiring
as a subroutine an efficient procedure for finding a "one-sided"
minimum of the given function (in the sense described later) on
an arbitrary ray in the space of problem variables. In other
words, a procedure is required which will efficiently find a
certain kind of approximate minimum, if such exists, of any convex, piecewise-linear function f of a single variable. Further,
in the given context of large-scale linear programming, the
function f cannot be explicitly described: rather, given any
value x of its argument, one can readily calculate $f(x)$ and one
support of the graph of f--that is, a "slope", denoted here by
$f'(x)$, such that

$$f(y) \geq f(x) + f'(x)(y - x) \qquad \text{for all } y$$

--but no more. The kind of function handled here is unusual in
one respect: $f'(x)$ is *not* continuous. Consequently, a method
designed for the more usual problem, in which $f'(x)$ is continuous,
does not work well in this case.

---

*Research partially sponsored by the Air Force Office of Scientific
Research, U.S. Air Force, under Contract f49620-77-C-0014. The
United States Government is authorized to reproduce and distribute
reprints for governmental purposes notwithstanding any copyright
notation hereon.

The algorithm below accomplishes the required end with what we believe to be near the smallest required computational effort.

PROBLEM STATEMENT

The piecewise-linear (more properly, piecewise-affine) function f is defined for all $x \geq 0$ by

$$f(x) = \text{Max } \{a_i x + b_i : i = 1,\ldots,I\} \quad , \qquad (1)$$

where, for each i, a_i and b_i are real numbers. The quantities a_i and b_i are not explicitly given: rather we suppose that we have a procedure which, for any $x \geq 0$, determines the value $f(x)$ and some a_i, b_i for which $f(x) = a_i x + b_i$. We denote that a_i by $f'(x)$. To simplify notation below we will suppose that $f(0) = 0$, and also that $M = f'(0) < 0$ (since, otherwise x=0 is trivially the minimizer).

We know that exact solution of the univariate minimization problem is not needed for success of the overall procedure of which it is a subroutine. Much computational labor can be saved by requiring only that the two following conditions be satisfied by the approximate minimizer x:

(a) $f(x) \leq Mm_2 x$,

(b) $f'(x) \geq Mm_1$.

(The constants m_1 and m_2 must satisfy the relations $0 < m_2 < m_1 < 1.0$.) Our goal is thus to find $x \geq 0$, $f(x)$, and $f'(x)$ satisfying (a) and (b). The "one-sided" nature of the requirement (b) is distinctive for the kind of problem of interest here, as opposed to the more usual requirement

$$|f'(x)| \leq m_1 |M| \quad ;$$

For efficiency, this problem needs a substantially different algorithm from that used if the latter requirement must be met.

Using the convexity of f it is easy to show that the two
functions

$$f(x)/x \ , \qquad f'(x)$$

are nondecreasing; so the set of all x satisfying (a) is an interval of the form [0,A] (where A=0 or A=∞ are both possible), and
the set of all x satisfying (b) is the form [B,∞) (with the same
possibilities for B). If A=∞ then (a) holds for all x, and our
procedure will generate a sequence of values of x tending to in-
finity, so that f(x) will tend to -∞. Otherwise it is easy to
show that B ≤ A, so that the two intervals overlap. The algorithm
below finds a point in that overlap.

ALGORITHM

When f and f' are evaluated for some value of x, the data
are recorded in the form of the triple (x, f(x), f'(x)). Supposing
terminal data (i.e., satisfying both (a) and (b) above) not to
have been found, L will denote the most recent triple evaluated
for which x lies in the interval [0,A], LL the previous such
triple, and R the most recent, if any, for the interval [B,∞).
Li(x,y,m) will denote the line of slope m passing through the
point (x,y); thus Li(L) is a line of slope f'(x) passing through
a point (x,f(x)). The "stepping factor" E is some number greater
than one; we have found the value E=6 useful. Component j of a
triple like L will be denoted L[j], as in the APL language. The
relations LL[1] ≤ L[1] < R[1] will hold throughout the course of
the algorithm.

It is supposed that a "starting" value x > 0 has been provided for the algorithm. Initially L and LL are set to (0,0,f'(0))
and R to (∞,∞,∞). The algorithm consists in execution of the
steps below in order (except where "go to" intervenes).

1.1 Evaluate f(x), f'(x).
1.2 If (a) does not hold, go to 4.
1.3 If (b) holds, terminate; x,f,f' is the solution.

2.1 Set LL to L.

2.2 Set L to (x,f(x), f'(x)).

2.3 If R[1] < ∞, go to 5.

3. (Extrapolation) Use linear extrapolation on the slopes LL[3], L[3] to determine the value x* (which may be ∞) at which f'(x*) should vanish. Set x to Min {x*,x + E(x - LL[1])}. Go to 1.1.

4. Set R to (x, f(x), f'(x)).

5. If the point (L(1), L(2)) is on the line Li(R), terminate; the solution is (L[1], L[2], R[3]).

6.1 Set x to the abscissa of the intersection of the lines Li(L), Li(R).

6.2 If R[3] ≥ 0, go to 1.

7.1 Set x to the larger of x and the abscissa of the intersection of the line Li(0,0,-m_2) with the line passing through (L[1],L[2]) and (R[1],R[2]). Go to 1.

Notes

- Step 3: x* is determined by the calculation: if LL[3] ≥ L[3], set x* = ∞. Otherwise

$$x* = (f'(x)\ LL[1] - x\ LL[3])/(f'(x) - LL[3]) \quad .$$

- Step 5: The point (L[1],L[2]) is on Li(R) when L[2] = R[2] + R[3] (R[1]-L[1]). In that case, Li(L[1],L[2],R[3]) is a support of f at L just as Li(L) is, and since R[3] ≥ L[3], the former is preferable.

- Step 6.1: x is given by the formula

$$(L[2] - R[2] + R[1]R[3] - L[1]L[3])/(R[3] - L[3]) \quad .$$

- Step 7.1: The desired abscissa is

$$(L[1]R[2] - R[1]L[2])/(R[2] - L[2] + m_2(R[1] - L[1])) \quad .$$

THE METHOD OF PARAMETRIC DECOMPOSITION IN MATHEMATICAL PROGRAMMING: THE NONCONVEX CASE

Jacques Gauvin

1. INTRODUCTION

We consider a large mathematical program which may be written in the following general formulation:

$$(P_0) \begin{cases} \max\ f(x,y,z) \\ \text{subject to } g_i(x,y) \leq 0 \quad,\quad i = 1,\dots,m \\ \qquad\qquad h_j(x,z) = 0 \quad,\quad j = 1,\dots,p \\ \qquad\qquad l_k(y,z) \leq 0 \quad,\quad k = 1,\dots,r \end{cases}$$

where $x \in R^n$, $y \in R^s$, $z \in R^t$. It is expected here that the objective function f and the constraints g_i, h_j are decomposable in their arguments x, y, and z and that the optimization is easy when y and z are held fixed.

Essentially in the method of parametric decomposition [3] or the method of primal decomposition by resource allocation [6], [15,16] the variables y and z are considered as parameters and are held fixed at the first optimization level where the following problem in x is solved by a standard NLP method:

$$(P_1) \begin{cases} \max\ f(x;y,z) \\ \text{subject to } g_i(x,y) \leq 0 \quad,\quad i = 1,\dots,m \\ \qquad\qquad h_j(x,a) = 0 \quad,\quad j = 1,\dots,p \end{cases}.$$

Let
$$S(y) = \{x \in R^n \mid g_i(x,y) \leq 0 \quad,\quad i = 1,\dots,m\}$$

$$T(z) = \{x \in R^n \mid h_j(x,z) = 0 \quad,\quad j = 1,\dots,p\}$$

and $U(y,z) = S(y) \cap T(z)$ be the feasible set for (P_1). The optimal value of (P_1) is given by

$$
v(y,z) = \begin{cases} \max\limits_{x \in U(y,z)} f(x,y,z) & \text{if} \quad U(y,z) \neq \phi \\ -\infty & \text{if} \quad U(y,z) = \phi \end{cases}
$$

which is called the extremal-value function.

$$
P(y,z) = \{\overline{x} \in U(y,z) \,|\, f(\overline{x},y,z) = v(y,z)\}
$$

is the set of optimal solutions for (P_1). $V = \{(y,z)\,|\,U(y,z) \neq \phi\}$ is the set of feasible parameters for (P_1).

At the second level, a postoptimization is performed on the feasible parameters

$$
(P_2) \begin{cases} \max v(y,z) \\ \text{subject to} \quad (y,z) \in V \\ \qquad\qquad l_k(y,z) \leq 0 \quad , \quad k = 1,\ldots,r \quad . \end{cases}
$$

In this method of decomposition-coordination by resource allocation, an optimal solution of subproblem (P_1) always gives at least a feasible solution to the original problem (P_0). Such is not the case in a dual-type method such as that of decomposition-coordination by prices (see Lasdon [9]) where a feasible solution of the original problem will only be attained, in general, at an optimal solution.

Under convexity assumptions, the extremal-value function $v(y,z)$ is concave and subdifferentiable, and some methods have been proposed to solve the problem (see, for example, [15,6,8]. A description of the first two works can be found in [9] Chapter 9).

To our knowledge, it seems that recent methods of nondifferentiable convex optimization [17,10] have not been applied to the problem of parametric decomposition.

It is not the purpose of this paper to survey the results
and methods of convex parametric decomposition, but rather to
see what can be done in the nonconvex case. To make the presen-
tation more simple, we will assume

$$f(x,y,z) = f(x)$$

$$g_i(x,y) = g_i(x) - y_i$$

$$h_j(x,y) = h_j(x) - z_j \ .$$

The extension of results to the more general problem can be easily
obtained.

First some results from [5] are presented from which a locally
Lipschitz property for the extremal-value function is derived.
Also an estimation of the generalized gradient of this function
is obtained. Maybe these results can be useful for designing
a method to solve the nonconvex and nondifferentiable second
level optimization problem.

Some results are already available in that direction. F.H.
Clarke [2] has given optimality conditions that can be applied
to the postoptimization problem. Also some algorithms have been
proposed for optimizing nondifferentiable nonconvex functions;
see [12] for such a proposal and a review of others.

In the sequel all functions defining program (P_0) are assumed
continuously differentiable.

2. A LOCALLY LIPSCHITZ PROPERTY FOR THE EXTREMAL-VALUE
   FUNCTION

Let $\bar{y}, \bar{z}$ be some feasible parameters for problem (P_0). For
$\bar{x}$, a local maximum of (P_1), let $I(\bar{x}; \bar{y}, \bar{z}) = \{i \mid g_i(\bar{x}) = \bar{y}_i\}$ be the
set of active inequality constraints and $K(\bar{x}; \bar{y}, \bar{z})$ be the set of
Kuhn-Tucker vectors corresponding to $\bar{x}$, that is the set of (u,v)
$\in R^m \times R^p$ such that

$$
\left\{
\begin{array}{l}
\nabla f(\bar{x}) = \sum_{i=1}^{m} u_i \, \nabla g_i(\bar{x}) + \sum_{j=1}^{p} v_j \, \nabla h_j(\bar{x}) \\[1.5em]
u_i \geq 0 \qquad\qquad i = 1,..,m \\[1.5em]
u_i(g_i(\bar{x}) - \bar{y}_i) = 0 \quad .
\end{array}
\right.
$$

Let

$$
K(\bar{y},\bar{z}) = \bigcup_{\bar{x} \, \in \, P(\bar{y},\bar{z})} K(\bar{x};\bar{y},\bar{z})
$$

be the set of all multipliers corresponding to $(\bar{y},\bar{z})$.

The directional derivative of $v(y,z)$ at $(\bar{y},\bar{z})$, for a direction $d = (d^1,d^2) \in R^m \times R^p$, $\|d\| = 1$, is

$$
v'(\bar{y},\bar{z};d) = \lim_{t \downarrow 0} \frac{v(\bar{y}+td^1,\bar{z}+td^2) - v(\bar{y},\bar{z})}{t} \quad .
$$

We will also consider lim inf and lim sup for the right-hand side expression. Examples show that these limits can be infinite if for some $\bar{x} \in P(\bar{y},\bar{z})$, $K(\bar{x};\bar{y},\bar{z})$ is empty or unbounded. To avoid this situation we assume at $\bar{x}$ the Mangasarian-Fromowitz constraint qualification, denoted (CQ1).

$$
\text{(CQ1)} \left\{
\begin{array}{l}
\text{(i)} \quad \text{There exists a } w \in R^n \text{ such that} \\[1em]
\qquad\qquad \nabla g_i(\bar{x}) \cdot w < 0 \quad , \quad i \in I(\bar{x};\bar{y},\bar{z}) \\[1em]
\qquad\qquad \nabla h_j(\bar{x}) \cdot w = 0 \quad , \quad j = 1,\ldots,p \quad . \\[1em]
\text{(ii)} \quad \text{The gradients } \{\nabla h_j(\bar{x})\}, \; j = 1,\ldots,p \\
\qquad\quad \text{are linearly independent.}
\end{array}
\right.
$$

In the absence of equality constraints, (CQ1) is equivalent to the Cottle constraint qualification: the system

$$\sum_{i \in I(\bar{x};\bar{y},\bar{z})} u_i \, \nabla g_i(\bar{x}) = 0 \quad , \quad u_i \geq 0$$

has no nonzero solution. If the g_i are convex and the h_j affine, (CQ1) is the well-known Slater condition.

This regularity condition has the following nice property (see [4 or 5]).

Lemma 2.1

Let $\bar{x}$ be a local maximum. Then $K(\bar{x};\bar{y},\bar{z})$ is a nonempty, convex and *compact* set if and only if (CQ1) is satisfied at $\bar{x}$.

The presence of equality constraints may cause the set $U(y,z)$ to be empty near $(\bar{y},\bar{z})$. The next lemma gives a condition to rule out this situation [5, Lemma 2.5].

Lemma 2.2

If (CQ1) is satisfied at some $\bar{x} \in P(\bar{y},\bar{z})$ then $U(y,z)$ is not empty near $(\bar{y},\bar{z})$.

Conditions to have the function $v(y,z)$ continuous are given in the following [5, Theorem 2.6].

Theorem 2.3

If $U(\bar{y},\bar{z})$ is nonempty and $U(y,z)$ is uniformly compact near $(\bar{y},\bar{z})$ then $U(y,z)$ and $v(y,z)$ are upper semicontinuous at $(\bar{y},\bar{z})$. Furthermore if (CQ1) holds at some $\bar{x} \in P(\bar{y},\bar{z})$ then $v(y,z)$ is also lower semicontinuous at $(\bar{y},\bar{z})$.

The (CQ1) regularity condition has the advantage of being preserved in a neighborhood of $(\bar{y},\bar{z})$ [5, Corollary 2.10].

Theorem 2.4

If in Theorem 2.3, (CQ1) holds at every $\bar{x} \in P(\bar{y},\bar{z})$, then there exists a $\delta > 0$, such that for all (y,z) satisfying

$\|(y,z) - (\bar{y},\bar{z})\| \leq \delta$, (CQ1) holds also at each $x \in P(y,z)$, the point-to-set map $K(y,z)$ is upper semi-continuous at $(\bar{y},\bar{z})$ and $K(y,z)$ is uniformly compact near $(\bar{y},\bar{z})$. More precisely, this result means that for any sequence $\{(y^n,z^n)\}$, $(y^n,z^n) \to (\bar{y},\bar{z})$, there exist $(u^n,v^n) \in K(y^n,z^n)$, a subsequence $\{(u^m,v^m)\}$ and a $(\bar{u},\bar{v}) \in K(\bar{y},\bar{z})$ such that $(u^m,v^m) \to (\bar{u},\bar{v})$.

It should be noted that $K(y,z)$ is not necessarily lower semicontinuous at $(\bar{y},\bar{z})$ under the assumptions of Theorem 2.4.

The next result gives bounds for the potential directional derivatives of $v(y,z)$. It does not require any second-order assumptions [5, Theorem 3.3].

Theorem 2.5

Suppose that $U(\bar{y},\bar{z})$ is nonempty, $u(y,z)$ is uniformly compact near $(\bar{y},\bar{z})$ and (CQ1) holds at some $\bar{x} \in P(\bar{y},\bar{z})$, then for any direction d

$$\min_{(u,v) \in K(\bar{x};\bar{y},\bar{z})} \{u \cdot d^1 + v \cdot d^2\}$$

$$\leq \liminf_{t \downarrow 0} \frac{v(\bar{y}+td^1, \bar{z}+td^2) - v(\bar{y},\bar{z})}{t} .$$

Furthermore, if we assume that (CQ1) holds at every $\bar{x} \in P(\bar{y},\bar{z})$ then

$$\max_{\bar{x} \in P(\bar{y},\bar{z})} \min_{(u,v) \in K(\bar{x};\bar{y},\bar{z})} \{u \cdot d^1 + v \cdot d^2\}$$

$$\leq \liminf_{t \downarrow 0} \frac{v(\bar{y}+td^1, \bar{z}+td^2) - v(\bar{y},\bar{z})}{t}$$

$$\leq \limsup_{t \downarrow 0} \frac{v(\bar{y}+td^1, \bar{z}+td^2) - v(\bar{y},\bar{z})}{t}$$

$$\leq \max_{\bar{x} \in P(\bar{y},\bar{z})} \quad \max_{(u,v) \in K(\bar{x};\bar{y},\bar{z})} \{u \cdot d^1 + v \cdot d^2\} \quad .$$

The bounds given in Theorem 2.5 are sharp: there are examples for which the directional derivatives of $v(y,z)$ exist at $(\bar{y},\bar{z})$ with the upper bound attained for a direction d_1, the lower bound attained for some other d_2, and a value strictly in between for a different d_3 (see [5, example 3.1]).

If in Theorem 2.5, we replace (CQ1) by the following more restrictive regularity condition.

(CQ2) $\begin{cases} \text{The gradients } \{\nabla g_i(\bar{x}), \nabla h_j(\bar{x})\}, \ i \in I(\bar{x};\bar{y},\bar{z}), \ j = 1,\ldots,p, \\ \text{are linearly independent.} \end{cases}$

then the directional derivative exists and is given by

$$v'(\bar{x},\bar{y};d) = \max_{\bar{x} \in P(\bar{y},\bar{z})} \{\bar{u} \cdot d^1 + \bar{v} \cdot d^2\} \qquad (2.6)$$

where $(\bar{u},\bar{v})$ is the unique multiplier vector corresponding to $\bar{x}$.

Under convexity assumptions, we can obtain the following corollary of Theorem 2.5 [5, Corollary 3.5]; [7].

Corollary 2.7

Suppose the functions f, $\{g_i\}$, $i = 1,\ldots,m$ are convex and $\{h_j\}$ are affine. If $U(\bar{y},\bar{z})$ is nonempty, $U(y,z)$ is uniformly compact near $(\bar{y},\bar{z})$ and (CQ1) (which is then equivalent to the Slater condition) is satisfied for each $\bar{x} \in P(\bar{y},\bar{z})$, then $v(y,z)$ has a directional derivative for any direction d at $(\bar{y},\bar{z})$ and

$$v'(\bar{y},\bar{z};d) = \max_{\bar{x} \in P(\bar{y},\bar{z})} \quad \min_{(u,v) \in K(\bar{x};\bar{y},\bar{z})} \{u \cdot d^1 + v \cdot d^2\} \quad .$$

From Theorem 2.4 and Theorem 2.5, it is possible to obtain a locally Lipschitz property for the extremal-value function.

Theorem 2.8

Suppose that $U(\bar{y},\bar{z})$ is nonempty, $U(y,z)$ is uniformly compact near $(\bar{y},\bar{z})$ and (CQ1) holds at every $\bar{x} \in P(\bar{y},\bar{z})$; then there exists a δ-neighborhood $N_\delta(\bar{y},\bar{z})$ and a finite K such that for any (y_1,z_1), $(y_2,z_2) \in N_\delta(\bar{y},\bar{z})$

$$|v(y_2,z_2) - v(y_1,z_1)| \leq K \|(y_2,z_2) - (y_1,z_1)\| \ .$$

Proof

From Theorem 2.4, the regularity condition (CQ1) remains valid at every $(y,z) \in N_\varepsilon(\bar{y},\bar{z})$, for some $\varepsilon > 0$, with the set of multipliers $K(y,z)$ uniformly bounded. Therefore, for some δ, $0 < \delta < \varepsilon$, Theorem 2.5 is valid at any $(y,z) \in N_\delta(\bar{y},\bar{z})$, and, for any direction $d = (d^1,d^2)$, $\|d\| = 1$, there exists some finite K_1 and K_2 such that

$$K_1 \leq \liminf_{t \downarrow 0} \ [v(y+td^1,z+td^2) - v(y,z)]/t$$

$$\leq \limsup_{t \downarrow 0} \ [v(y+td^1,z+td^2) - v(y,z)]/t \leq K_2 \qquad (2.9)$$

For (y^2,z^2), $(y^1,z^1) \in N_\delta(\bar{y},\bar{z})$, write (y^2,z^2), $- (y^1,z^1)$ $= \lambda(d^1,d^2)$ where $\|(d^1,d^2)\| = 1$ and $\lambda = \|(y^2,z^2) - (y^1,z^1)\|$. From (2.9) it follows that the function $v(y^1+td^1,z^1+td^2)$ is Lipschitz continuous on the ray d, for $t \in [0,\lambda]$, hence absolutely continuous on that ray. Therefore its derivative exists almost everywhere and we can write

$$v(y^1+\lambda d^1,z^1+\lambda d^2) - v(y^1,z^1) = \int_0^\lambda \frac{d}{dt} v(y^1+td^1,z^1+td^2) \ dt \ .$$

This derivative, when it exists, is equal to the right derivative, which is the directional derivative $v'(y^1+td^1,z^1+td^2;d)$. From (2.9) we then obtain

$$K_1\lambda \le v(y^2,z^2) - v(y^1,z^1) \le K_2\lambda$$

and the result follows with $K = \max\{|K_1|,|K_2|\}.\|$

Stern and Topkis [14] have obtained the previous result for a program without equality constraints

$$\begin{cases} \max\ f(x) \\ \text{subject to } g_i(x) \le y_i \ , \qquad\qquad i = 1,\ldots,m \end{cases}$$

assuming that the functions $g_i(x)$ have continuous second derivatives.

F.H. Clarke [2] also considers the problem

$$(P_s) \begin{cases} \min\ g_0(x) \\ \text{subject to } g_i(x) \le s_i \ , \qquad\qquad i = 1,\ldots,m \end{cases}$$

where he defines (P_s) to be "calm" if the extremal-value function

$$\phi(s) = \inf\{g_0(x)\,|\,g_i(x) \le s_i \ , \qquad\qquad i = 1,\ldots,m\}$$

is finite, and if

$$\liminf_{s'\to s} \frac{[\phi(s') - \phi(s)]}{\|s'-s\|} > -\infty$$

The program (P_s) is also defined to be "normal" if the Kuhn-Tucker conditions hold at every optimal point $\bar{x}$ of (P_s). In fact, Clarke does not assume that the functions $g_i(x)$ are differentiable and he gives some generalized Kuhn-Tucker conditions which reduce to the usual ones when differentiability is assumed. Then he shows that if (P_s) is "calm" then (P_s) is normal. The converse of this result is not valid unless (P_s) is assumed "normal" with bounded multipliers. He also shows that on a neighborhood S of

0 where $\phi(s)$ is finite, P(s) is "calm" and "normal" for almost all s in S. The following example shows that the "almost all s" is meaningful.

Example 2.10

$$(P_s) \quad \left\{ \begin{array}{l} \min\ g_0(x) = -x \\[2ex] \text{subject to } g_1(x) = x^3 \leq s \end{array} \right.$$

Then $\phi(s) = -s^{1/3}$ and (P_s) is either "normal" or "calm" at s = 0.

3. THE GENERALIZED GRADIENT OF THE EXTREMAL-VALUE FUNCTION

For the previous section, we have conditions to guarantee the extremal-value function v(y,z) to be Lipschitz in some ball about $(\bar{y},\bar{z})$. Following Clarke [1] the gradient $\nabla v(y,z)$ then exists almost everywhere in that ball (Rademacher's theorem).

Definition 3.1 [1]

The *generalized gradient* of v(y,z) at $(\bar{y},\bar{z})$ denoted $\partial v(\bar{y},\bar{z})$, is the convex hull of the set of limits of the form $\lim \nabla v(\bar{y}+h_n,\bar{z}+k_n)$, where $(h_n,k_n) \to (0,0)$.

$\partial v(\bar{y},\bar{z})$ is a nonempty convex compact set. The *generalized directional derivative* of v(y,z) at $(\bar{y},\bar{z})$ for the direction $d = (d^1,d^2) \in R^m \times R^p$ is

$$v^0(\bar{y},\bar{z};d) = \limsup_{\substack{(y,z)\to(\bar{y},\bar{z}) \\ t\downarrow 0}} [v(y+td^1,z+td^2) - v(y,z)]/t \ .$$

Then

$$v^0(\bar{y},\bar{z};d) = \max\{g^1 \cdot d^1 + g^2 \cdot d^2 | (g^1,g^2) \in \partial v(\bar{y},\bar{z})\} \ ,$$

that is, $v^0(\bar{y},\bar{z};\cdot)$ is the *support function* of $\partial v(\bar{y},\bar{z})$.

We can obtain, under the assumptions of Theorem 2.8, the following estimation for the generalized gradient of the extremal-value function.

Theorem 3.2

Suppose that $U(\bar{y},\bar{z})$ is nonempty, $U(y,z)$ is uniformly compact near $(\bar{y},\bar{z})$ and (CQ1) holds at every optimal point $\bar{x} \in P(\bar{y},\bar{z})$. Then the generalized gradient of $v(y,z)$ at $(\bar{y},\bar{z})$ is contained in the convex hull of all the Kuhn-Tucker multipliers corresponding to the optimal points; that is $\partial v(\bar{y},\bar{z}) \subseteq$ co $K(\bar{y},\bar{z})$.

Proof

Take a sequence $\{(y^n,z^n)\}$, $(y^n,z^n) \to (\bar{y},\bar{z})$ where $\nabla v(y^n,z^n)$ exists. For any direction $d = (d^1,d^2) \in R^m \times R^p$ we have, by Theorem 2.4, that (CQ1) still holds in some neighborhood of $(\bar{y},\bar{z})$, and we have, by Theorem 2.5,

$$\nabla v(y^n,z^n) \cdot d = \lim_{t \downarrow 0} [v(y^n+td^1,z^n+td^2) - v(y^n,z^n)]/t$$

$$\leq \max_{(u,v) \in K(y^n,z^n)} [u \cdot d^1 + v \cdot d^2]$$

$$= [u^n \cdot d^1 + v^n \cdot d^2]$$

for some $(u^n,v^n) \in K(y^n,z^n)$. Again from Theorem 2.4, there exists a subsequence $\{(u^m,v^m)\}$, a $(\bar{u},\bar{v}) \in K(\bar{y},\bar{z})$ such that $(u^m,v^m) \to (\bar{u},\bar{v})$. Taking the limit on both sides we obtain by [13, Theorem 32.2],

$$[\lim \nabla v(y^n,z^n)] \cdot d \leq \bar{u} \cdot d^1 + \bar{v} \cdot d^2$$

$$\leq \max_{(u,v) \in K(\bar{y},\bar{z})} [u \cdot d^1 + v \cdot d^2] \ .$$

$$= \max_{(u,v) \in \text{co } K(\bar{y},\bar{z})} [u \cdot d^1 + v \cdot d^2] \ .$$

Since this result holds for every direction d, we have, by [13, Theorem 13.1],

$$\lim \nabla v(y^n, z^n) \in co\ K(\bar{y}, z) \quad .$$

This with Definition 3.1 gives the result. ‖

If the directional derivative $v'(\bar{y}, \bar{z}; d)$ exists and is equal to $v^0(y, z; d)$ for every direction d, then $v(y, z)$ is said to be *quasidifferentiable* at $(\bar{y}, \bar{z})$ (see [11]).

Corollary 3.3

If in Theorem 3.2 the regularity condition (CQ1) is replaced by (CQ2) (see (2.6)), then $\partial v(\bar{y}, \bar{z}) = co\ K(\bar{y}, \bar{z})$ and $v(y, z)$ is quasidifferentiable at $(\bar{y}, \bar{z})$.

Proof

For any $(u, v) \in K(\bar{y}, \bar{z})$, we have

$$u \cdot d^1 + v \cdot d^2 \leq \max_{(u, v) \in K(\bar{y}, \bar{z})} [u \cdot d^1 + v \cdot d^2]$$

$$= v'(\bar{y}, \bar{z}; d) \qquad \text{by } (2.6)$$

$$\leq v^0(\bar{y}, \bar{z}; d) \quad ;$$

hence, by [13, Theorem 13.1], $(u, v) \in \partial v(\bar{y}, \bar{z})$ and $K(\bar{y}, \bar{z}) \subseteq \partial v(\bar{y}, \bar{z})$.

By Theorem 3.2, $\partial v(\bar{y}, \bar{z}) = co\ K(\bar{y}, \bar{z})$. Therefore we have, for every direction d,

$$v^0(\bar{y}, \bar{z}; d) = \max_{(u, v) \in co\ K(\bar{y}, \bar{z})} [u \cdot d^1 + v \cdot d^2]$$

$$= \max_{(u, v) \in K(\bar{y}, \bar{z})} [u \cdot d^1 + v \cdot d^2] = v'(\bar{y}, \bar{z}; d)$$

by [13, Theorem 32.2] and (2.6). ‖

The next example illustrates the previous result.

Example 3.4

$$\max f = \begin{cases} x^3 & \text{if } x \geq 0 \\ x^2 & \text{if } x \leq 0 \end{cases}$$

subject to $g = x^2 - 1 \leq y$

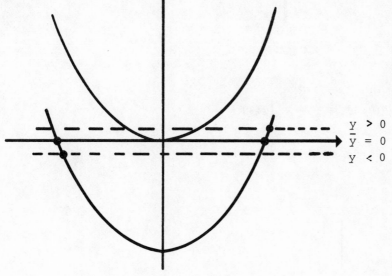

At $\bar{y} = 0$, the maximum occurs at $\bar{x}_1 = 1$ with multiplier $\bar{u}_1 = 3/2$ and at $\bar{x}_2 = -1$ with multiplier $\bar{u}_2 = 1$ where (CQ2) is satisfied at both points.

For $y > 0$, the maximizer is $+\sqrt{1+y}$, and for $y < 0$, the maximizer is $-\sqrt{1+y}$; hence the extremal-value function is

$$v(y) = \begin{cases} (1+y)^{3/2} & \text{if } y > 0 \\ (1+y) & \text{if } y < 0 \end{cases}$$

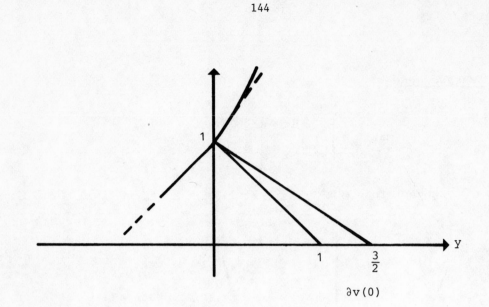

$\partial v(0)$

Therefore

$$v'(0;1) = \frac{3}{2} = v^0(0;1)$$

$$v'(0;-1) = -1 = v^0(0;-1)$$

and

$$\partial v(y) = \begin{cases} \dfrac{3}{2} & \text{if } y > 0 \\[2mm] [1,\dfrac{3}{2}] & \text{if } y = 0 \\[2mm] 1 & \text{if } y < 0 \end{cases}$$

The next example shows that under assumption (CQ1) the extremal-value function is not necessary quasidifferentiable.

Example 3.5

$$\max f = x_2$$

$$\text{subject to } g_1 = x_2 + x_1^2 \le y_1$$

$$g_2 = x_2 - x_1^2 \le y_2$$

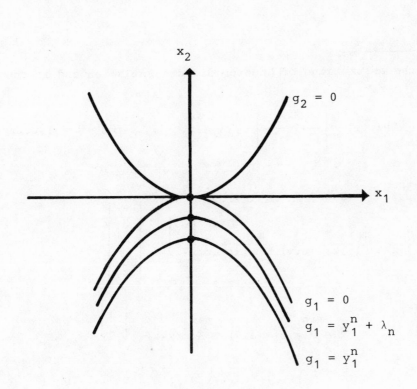

At $\bar{y} = (0,0)$, the maximum occurs at $\bar{x} = (0,0)$ where (CQ1) holds with the set of multipliers

$$K(\bar{x};0) = \{(u_1,u_2) \,|\, u_1 + u_2 = 1, \; u_1 \geq 0, \; u_2 \geq 0\} \quad .$$

For the direction $d = (1,0)$, $v'(0;d) = \frac{1}{2}$. Now take a sequence $\{y^n, \lambda_n\}$ where $y^n = (y_1^n, 0)$, $y_1^n < 0$, $y_1^n \to 0$, $\lambda_n \downarrow 0$, $\lambda_n < |y_1^n|$; then

$$[v(y^n + \lambda_n d) - v(y^n)]/\lambda_n = [y_1^n + \lambda_n - y_1^n]/\lambda_n = 1 \leq v^0(0;d) \quad ,$$

and therefore $v^0(0;d) \neq v'(0;d)$ and $v(y)$ is not quasidifferentiable at $\bar{y} = 0$.

The next results characterize the gradients of $v(y,z)$ when they are assumed to exist.

Corollary 3.6

If the assumptions of Theorem 3.2 are satisfied and if the gradient

$$\nabla v(\bar{y},\bar{z}) = \left[\frac{\partial v}{\partial \bar{y}_i}, \frac{\partial v}{\partial \bar{z}_j}\right] , \qquad i = 1,\ldots,m ; \quad j = 1,\ldots,p,$$

exists, then

$$\max_{\bar{x} \in P(\bar{y},\bar{z})} \min_{(u,v) \in K(\bar{x};\bar{y},\bar{z})} \begin{bmatrix} u_i \\ v_j \end{bmatrix} \leq \begin{bmatrix} \dfrac{\partial v}{\partial \bar{y}_i} \\ \dfrac{\partial v}{\partial \bar{z}_j} \end{bmatrix}$$

$$\leq \min_{\bar{x} \in P(\bar{y},\bar{z})} \max_{(u,v) \in K(\bar{x};\bar{y},\bar{z})} \begin{bmatrix} u_i \\ v_j \end{bmatrix}$$

$$i = 1,\ldots,m ; \quad j = 1,\ldots,p .$$

Proof

For any direction d we have, by Theorem 2.5,

$$\nabla v(\bar{y},\bar{z}) \cdot d = v'(\bar{y},\bar{z};d)$$

$$\geq \max_{\bar{x} \in P(\bar{y},\bar{z})} \min_{(u,v) \in K(\bar{x};\bar{y},\bar{z})} [u \cdot d^1 + v \cdot d^2] .$$

Hence for the direction -d,

$$\nabla v(\bar{y},\bar{z}) \cdot (-d) \geq \max \min - [u \cdot d^1 + v \cdot d^2] ,$$

which implies

$$\nabla v(\bar{y},\bar{z}) \cdot d \leq \min_{\bar{x} \in P(\bar{y},\bar{z})} \max_{(u,v) \in K(\bar{x};\bar{y},\bar{z})} [u \cdot d^1 + v \cdot d^2] .$$

These two inequalities taken with the directions d equal to the unit vectors in $R^m \times R^p$ give the results. ‖

Corollary 3.7

If in Corollary 3.6 the regularity condition (CQ1) is re-placed by (CQ2), then the set of multipliers is a singleton, that is $K(\bar{y},\bar{z}) = \{(\bar{u},\bar{v})\}$ and $\nabla v(\bar{y},\bar{z}) = (\bar{u},\bar{v})$.

Proof

Under (CQ2), for each $\bar{x} \in P(\bar{y},\bar{z})$, $K(\bar{x};\bar{y},\bar{z})$ is a singleton. From Corollary 3.6, we have

$$\max_{\bar{x} \in P(\bar{y},\bar{z})} u_i \leq \frac{\partial v}{\partial y_i} \leq \min_{\bar{x} \in P(\bar{y},\bar{z})} u_i , \qquad i = 1,\ldots,m,$$

which implies the result. (The same holds for $\frac{\partial v}{\partial z_j}$, $j = 1,\ldots,p$.)||

Recently R. Mifflin [11,12] has introduced the notion of semismooth and weakly upper semismooth functions. The defini-tions are the following.

Definition 3.8

A function $F:R^n \to R$ is *semismooth* at $\bar{x} \in R^n$ if

(i) F is Lipschitz on a ball about $\bar{x}$ and

(ii) for each direction $d \in R^n$ and for any sequences $\{t_k\} \subset R_+$, $\{\theta_k\} \subset R^n$ and $\{g_k\} \subset R^n$ such that $\{t_k\} \downarrow 0$, $\{\theta_k/t_k\} \to 0$ and $g_k \in \partial F(\bar{x}+t_k d+\theta_k)$ the sequence $\{g_k \cdot d\}$ has exactly one accumu-lation point.

Definition 3.9

$F: R^n \to R$ is *weakly upper semismooth* at $\bar{x}$ if the follow-ing conditions hold:

(i) F is Lipschitz on a ball about $\bar{x}$

(ii) for each direction $d \in R^n$

$$\liminf_{k \to \infty} g_k \cdot d \geq \limsup_{t \downarrow 0} [F(\bar{x}+td) - F(\bar{x})]/t$$

where $\{g_k\} \subset R^n$ is any sequence such that $g_k \in \partial F(\bar{x}+t_k d)$ and $\{t_k\} \subset R_+$ is any sequence such that $\{t_k\} \downarrow 0$.

In Example 3.5 it can be easily seen that the extremal-value function is weakly upper semismooth and even semismooth. At the present time, it is not known whether these properties are generally satisfied or not by the extremal-value function under the assumption of Theorem 3.2.

ACKNOWLEDGEMENT

The author would like to express his gratitude to Professor A.A. Goldstein for his helpful assistance in the proof of Theorem 2.8.

REFERENCES

[1] Clarke, F.H., Generalized Gradients and Applications, *Transactions of the American Mathematical Society*, 205 (1975), 247-262.

[2] Clark, F.H., A New Approach to Lagrange Multipliers, *Mathematics of Operations Research*, 1, 2 (1976), 165-174.

[3] Ermolev, Y.M., and L.G. Ermoleva, The Method of Parametric Decompositon, *Kibernetika* 9, 2 (1973), 66-69; *Cybernetics*, 9, 2, 262-266.

[4] Gauvin, J., A Necessary and Sufficient Condition to Have Bounded Multipliers in Nonconvex Programming, *Mathematical Programming*, 12, 1 (1977), 136-138.

[5] Gauvin, J., and J.W. Tolle, Differential Stability in Nonlinear Programming, *SIAM Journal on Control and Optimization*, 15, 2 (1977), 294-311.

[6] Geoffrion, A.M., Primal Resource Directive Approaches for Optimizing Nonlinear Decomposable Systems, *Operations Research*, 18, 3 (1970), 375-403.

[7] E.G. Gol'stein, *Theory of Convex Programming*, in Translation of Mathematical Monographs, Vol. 36, American Mathematical Society, Providence, R.I., 1972.

[8] Hogan, W.W., Directional Derivatives for Extremal Valued Functions with Applications to the Completely Convex Case, *Operations Research*, 21, 1 (1973), 188-209.

149

[9]   Lasdon, L.S., *Optimization Theory for Large Systems*,
      Macmillan, N.Y., 1970.

[10] Lemarechal, C., An Extension of Davidon Methods to Non-
      differentiable Problems, in M.L. Balinski and P. Wolfe,
      eds., *Nondifferentiable Optimization*, Mathematical
      Programming Study 3, North-Holland, Amsterdam, 1975,
      95-109.

[11] Mifflin, R., Semismooth and Semiconvex Functions in Con-
      strained Optimization, *Siam Journal on Control and
      Optimization*, 15, 6 (1976), 959-972.

[12] Mifflin, R., An Algorithm for Constrained Optimization
      with Semismooth Functions, *Mathematics of Optimization
      Research*, 2, 2 (1977), 191-207.

[13] Rockafellar, R.T., *Convex Analysis*, Princeton Univ. Press,
      Princeton, N.J., 1970.

[14] Stern, M.H., and D.M. Topkis, Rates of Stability in Nonlinear
      Programming, *Operations Research*, 24 (1976), 462-476.

[15] Silverman, G.J., Primal Decomposition of Mathematical
      Programs by Resource Allocation, I. Basic Theory and
      a Direction Finding Procedure, *Operations Research*,
      20, 1 (1972), 58-74.

[16] Silverman, G.J., Primal Decomposition of Mathematical
      Programs by Resource Allocation: II-Computational
      Algorithm with an Application to the Modular Design
      Problem, *Operations Research*, 20, 1 (1972), 75-93.

[17] Wolfe, P., A Method of Conjugate Subgradients for Minimiz-
      ing Nondifferentiable Functions, in M.L. Balinski
      and P. Wolfe, eds., *Nondifferentiable Optimization*,
      Mathematical Programming Study 3, North-Holland,
      Amsterdam, 1975, 145-173.

A SET OF NONSMOOTH OPTIMIZATION TEST PROBLEMS

Test Problem 1:   MAXQUAD

The objective function to be minimized is

$$f(x) = \max \{(A_k x, x) - (b_k, x) \mid k = 1, \ldots, 5\}$$

where

$$x \in R^{10} \ .$$

The (symmetric, diagonal dominating) matrices A_k, together with the vectors b_k, are given by the fancy formulae:

$$A_k(i,j) = e^{i/j} \cos (i,j) \sin (k) \qquad i < j$$

$$b_k(i) = e^{i/k} \sin (i.k) \ ,$$

and the diagonals of A_k are

$$A_k(i,i) = \frac{i}{10} \sin (k) + \sum_{j \neq i} A_k(i,j) \ .$$

The following naive FORTRAN program fills up the data for K MAX = 5, N = 10.

151

```
      do 30 k=1,kmax
      ak=float(k)
      do 10 i=1,n
      ai=float(i)
      do 10 j=i,n
      aj=float(j)
      a(k,i,j)=exp(ai/aj)*cos(ai*aj)*sin(ak)
      a(k,j,i)=a(k,i,j)
   10 continue
      do 20 i=1,n
      ai=float(i)
      f(k,i)=exp(ai/ak)*sin(ai*ak)
      a(k,i,i)=abs(sin(ak))*float(i)/float(n)
      do 20 j=1,n
      if(j.ne.i) a(k,i,i)=a(k,i,i)+abs(a(k,i,j))
   20 continue
   30 continue
```

For this particular problem, the optimal solution is

$$f^* = -0.8414$$

$$x^* = (-0.1263, -0.0346, -0.0067, 0.2668, 0.0673,$$
$$0.2786, 0.0744, 0.1387, 0.0839, 0.0385) \quad .$$

The following FORTRAN program computes the value of the objective, VAL, and a subgradient, G, at a given point, x.

```
      k0=0
      do 50 k=1,kmax
      fi=0.
      do 10 i=1,n
      z=x(i)
      fi=fi-f(k,i)*z
      do 10 j=1,n
   10 fi=fi+a(k,i,j)*x(j)*z
      if(k0.eq.0) go to 20
      if(fi.le.val) go to 50
   20 k0=k
      val=fi
   50 continue
      do 70 i=1,n
      z=-f(k0,i)
      do 60 j=1,n
   60 z=z+2.*a(k0,i,j)*x(j)
   70 g(i)=z
```

The standard starting point is $x_i = 1$ $i = 1,\ldots,n$, for which $f = 5337$. Another interesting starting point is $x = 0$, since f has a kink at this point ($f_k(0) = 0$ $k = 1,\ldots,k$ max).

Test Problem 2:   SHELL DUAL

This is the second problem of Colville, where all the con-
straints are penalized with an ℓ_1 penalty function (A.R. Colville:
A Comparative Study of Nonlinear Programming Codes, IBM, New York,
Scientific Report 320.2949 (1968)).

There are two groups of variables: x_i, $i = 1,\ldots,k=10$
and y_j, $j = 1,\ldots,m=5$.

The original problem from Colville is

$$\min \ 2 \sum_{j=1}^{m} d_j y_j^3 + (Cy,y) - (b,x)$$

$$(Ax)_j - 2(Cy)_j \leq e_j + 3d_j y_j^2 \qquad j = 1,\ldots,m$$

$$x \geq 0 \ , \qquad y \geq 0 \ .$$

Here we define the functions

$$P_j(x,y) = (Ax)_j - 2(Cy)_j - 3d_j y_j^2 - e_j$$

$$Q(x,y) = \sum_{i=1}^{k} \min(0,x_i) + \sum_{j=1}^{m} \min(0,y_j) \ ,$$

and the function to be minimized is

$$f(x,y) = 2 \left| \sum_{j=1}^{m} d_j y_j^3 \right| + (Cy,y) - (b,x)$$

$$+ \ 100 \left\{ \sum_{j=1}^{m} \max(0,P_j(x,y)) - Q(x,y) \right\} \ .$$

155

The vectors d, e, b and matrices A and C are given at the end
of this problem.

A program which computes the function f(x,y) and its
gradient is also given. In this program, the data m, k, d, b,
e, A, C, together with PENAL = 100 are supposed to be passed in
a COMMON block.

The variables x and y form a single vector X where

$$X(I) = y_i \quad i = 1,\ldots,m$$

$$X(M+I) = x_i \quad i = 1,\ldots,k \ .$$

The optimal point is f* = 32.3488

$$y^* = (0.3, \ 0.3335, \ 0.4, \ 0.4283, \ 0.224)$$

$$x^* = (0., \ 0., \ 5.1741, \ 0., \ 3.0611,$$
$$11.8396, \ 0., \ 0., \ 0.1039, \ 0.) \ .$$

The starting point is f = 2400.

$$y_j = 0.0001 \quad j = 1,\ldots,5$$

$$x_i = 0.0001 \quad i \neq 7$$

$$x_7 = 60 \ .$$

Data for SHELL DUAL

```
d =        4.     8.    10.     6.     2.

e =      -15.   -27.   -36.   -18.   -12.
```

		Matrix a			b
-16.	2.	0.	1.	0.	-40.
0.	-2.	0.	4.	2.	-2.
-3.5	0.	2.	0.	0.	-0.25
0.	-2.	0.	-4.	-1.	-4.
0.	-9.	-2.	1.	-2.8	-4.
2.	0.	-4.	0.	0.	-1.
-1.	-1.	-1.	-1.	-1.	-40.
-1.	-2.	-3.	-2.	-1.	-60.
1.	2.	3.	4.	5.	5.
1.	1.	1.	1.	1.	1.

Symmetric Matrix c

30.	-20.	-10.	32.	-10.
-20.	39.	-6.	-31.	32.
-10.	-6.	10.	-6.	-10.
32.	-31.	-6.	39.	-20.
-10.	32.	-10.	-20.	30.

Program for computing function and gradient in SHELL DUAL

```
          z=0.
          do 10 j=1,m
      10  z=z+d(j)*x(j)*x(j)*x(j)
          if (z.lt.0.) go to 30
          val=2.*z
          do 20 j=1,m
      20  g(j)=6.*d(j)*x(j)*x(j)
          go to 50
      30  val=-2.*z
          do 40 j=1,m
      40  g(j)=-6.*d(j)*x(j)*x(j)
c
      50  do 70 j=1,m
          z=0.
          do 60 i=1,m
      60  z=z+c(i,j)*x(i)
          val=val+z*x(j)
      70  g(j)=g(j)+2.*z
c
          do 80 i=1,k
          il=m+i
          val=val-b(i)*x(il)
      80  g(il)=-b(i)
c
c                   compute the constraints
c
          do 200 j=1,m
          z=-3.*d(j)*x(j)*x(j)-e(j)
          do 120 i=1,k
          il=m+i
     120  z=z+a(i,j)*x(il)
          do 140 i=1,m
     140  z=z-2.*c(i,j)*x(i)
          if(z.le.0.) go to 200
          val=val+penal*z
          g(j)=g(j)-6.*penal*d(j)*x(j)
          do 160 i=1,k
          il=m+i
     160  g(il)=g(il)+penal*a(i,j)
          do 180 i=1,m
     180  g(i)=g(i)-2.*penal*c(i,j)
     200  continue
c
c          now the nonnegativity constraints
c
          do 320 i=1,n
          if (x(i).ge.0.) go to 320
          val=val-penal*x(i)
          g(i)=g(i)-penal
     320  continue
```

Test Problem 3: EQUIL

The following nonconvex problem is a min-max formulation of an economic equilibrium problem in Scarf (The Approximation of Fixed Points of a Continuous Mapping, *SIAM Journal on Applied Mathematics*, 15 (1967), 1328-1343).

$$\text{Minimize } \{\max[f_i(x) : i = 1,2,\ldots,N] : \sum_{j=1}^{N} x_j = 1 ,$$

$$x_j \geq 0 , \; j = 1,2,\ldots,N\}$$

where

$$x \in R^N$$

$$f_i(x) = \sum_{\ell=1}^{NA} f_i^\ell(x) \qquad \text{for } i = 1,2,\ldots,N ,$$

$$f_i^\ell(x) = (A_{\ell i} \sum_{k=1}^{N} W_{\ell k} x_k) / (x_i^{B_\ell} \sum_{k=1}^{N} A_{\ell k} x_k^{1-B_\ell}) - W_{\ell i}$$

$$\text{for } \ell = 1,2,\ldots,NA .$$

The input data N, NA, $W_{\ell k}$, $A_{\ell k}$ and B are given below.

Data for EQUIL

N = 8   NA = 5

Matrix W

3.	1.	.1	.1	5.	.1	.1	6.
.1	10.	.1	.1	5.	.1	.1	.1
.1	9.	10.	.1	4.	.1	7.	.1
.1	.1	.1	10.	.1	3.	.1	.1
.1	.1	.1	.1	.1	.1	.1	11.

Matrix A

1.	1.	1.	1.	1.	1.	1.	1.
2.	.8	1.	.5	1.	1.	1.	1.
1.	1.2	.8	1.2	1.6	2.	.6	.1
2.	.1	.6	2.	1.	1.	1.	2.
1.2	1.2	.8	1.	1.2	.1	3.	4.

Vector b = [.5 1.2 .8 2. 1.5]

An interesting starting point is

$$x_j = .125 \text{ for all } j$$

where $f(x) = \max_i f_i(x)$ has the value 9.7878. The optimal value
of f is zero and occurs at a strictly positive point near

$$x = (.27, .03, .06, .09, .07, .31, .10, .07) \ .$$

The following FORTRAN SUBROUTINE CALCUL (x,G,VAL) requires the
data NA, N, A, W and B to be available in the common blocks
labelled ENTIER and REEL. It is useful when

$$(C) \quad \sum_{j=1}^{N} x_j = 1 \ .$$

If $x_j > 0$ for all j it returns the value of f in VAL and returns a projected (with respect to (C)) generalized gradient in G. Otherwise, it returns an arbitrarily large number in VAL and no useful G.

```
          SUBROUTINE CALCUL(X,G,VAL)
          COMMON /ENTIER/ NA,N
          COMMON /REEL/ A(5,10),W(5,10),B(5)
          COMMON /EXCESS/ ED(10),R(5,10),D(5,10),XB(5,10)
          DIMENSION X(10),G(10)
          VAL=1.E20
          DO 10 I=1,N
          ED(I)=0.
          G(I)=0.
    10 CONTINUE
          DO 100 L=1,NA
          SUMR=0.
          SUMD=0.
          DO 20 K=1,N
          IF(X(K).LE.0.)GO TO 400
          XB(L,K)=X(K)**B(L)
          SUMD=SUMD+A(L,K)*X(K)/XB(L,K)
    20 SUMR=SUMR+W(L,K)*X(K)
          DO 80 I=1,N
          D(L,I)=XB(L,I)*SUMD
          R(L,I)=A(L,I)*SUMR/D(L,I)
    80 ED(I)=ED(I)+R(L,I)-W(L,I)
   100 CONTINUE
          IMAX=1
          VAL=ED(1)
          DO 200 I=2,N
          IF (ED(I).LE.VAL) GO TO 200
          VAL=ED(I)
          IMAX=I
   200 CONTINUE
          SUM=0.
          DO 300 J=1,N
          DO 240 L=1,NA
          TLJ=A(L,J)*(1.-B(L))
          IF (J.EQ.IMAX) GO TO 230
          T=TLJ*XB(L,IMAX)/XB(L,J)
          GO TO 240
   230 T=TLJ+B(L)*D(L,J)/X(J)
   240 G(J)=G(J)+(A(L,IMAX)*W(L,J)-T*R(L,IMAX))/D(L,IMAX)
          SUM=SUM+G(J)
   300 CONTINUE
          SUM=SUM/FLOAT(N)
          DO 350 J=1,N
   350 G(J)=G(J)-SUM
   400 RETURN
          END
```

Test Problem 4:   TR48

This problem is the dual of a transportation problem with 48 sources and 48 destinations.   It was communicated to us by J.L. Goffin and the cost data is from M. Held, R.M. Karp: A Dynamic Programming Approach to Sequencing Problems, *J. Soc. Indust. Appl. Math.*, 10, 1 (1962), 196-210.

The objective to be minimized is

$$f(x) = -\{ \sum_{i=1}^{n} s_i x_i + \sum_{j=1}^{n} d_j \min_{i=1}^{n} (a_{ij} - x_i) \}$$

where n = 48.   See the following pages for the statements for computing the function and its gradient, for the data, and for the initial and optimal points.

The initialization x = 0 is standard.   The point "initial 2" is given by J.L. Goffin.   It has been computed by subgradient optimization.

Statements for computing function and gradient in TR48

```
        f=0.
        do 10 i=1,n
        g(i)=s(i)
 10     f=f+s(i)*x(i)
        do 50 j=1,n
        xmax=1.e30
        do 40 i=1,n
        z=a(i,j)-x(i)
        if(z.gt.xmax) go to 40
        xmax=z
        k=i
 40     continue
        g(k)=g(k)-d(j)
        f=f+d(j)*xmax
 50     continue
        f=-f
        do 70 i=1,n
 70     g(i)=-g(i)
```

Sources and destinations

```
vector s   22, 53, 64, 15, 66, 37, 16, 23, 67, 18, 52, 69,
           17, 29, 50, 13, 95, 34, 59, 36, 22, 94, 28, 34,
           36, 38, 55, 77, 45, 34, 32, 58, 30, 88, 74, 59,
           93, 54, 89, 30, 79, 46, 35, 41, 99, 52, 76, 93.

vector d   61, 67, 24, 84, 13, 86, 89, 46, 48, 50, 74, 75,
           88, 40, 29, 45, 32, 21, 61, 21, 51, 14, 89, 79,
           38, 20, 97, 19, 10, 73, 59, 92, 52, 66, 89, 65,
           63, 47,  7, 61, 87, 19, 36, 43,  9, 12,  8, 67.
```

Statements for reading the symmetric cost matrix A

```
  1 format((16f5.0))
    read 1, ((a(i-1,j),j=i,n),i=2,n)
    do 10 i=1,n
    a(i,i)=100000.
    do 10 j=1,i
    a(i,j)=a(j,i)
 10 continue
```

(data for A on next page)

Data for Cost Matrix in TR48

```
 273 1272  744 1138 1972 1580 1878 1539 1457  429 1129 1251 1421  588  334  837
1364  229  961  754 1169 1488  720 1280  816  664 1178  939 1698  983 1119 1029
1815  721 1753  330 1499 1107 1576  942  484  617  896 1184 1030 1718  604  999
 809  866 1722 1338 1640 1266 1185  440  894  992 1173  334  358  626 1124  358
 847  533  915 1219  481 1009  543  937  915  667 1441  812  848  776 1560  526
1494  598 1244 1304 1306  685  668  444 1157 1359 1176 1475  335 1519  140  937
 697  951  267  227 1229  587  369  554  721 1212  739  596 1291 1114  701  426
 285  676  155  456 1936  319  337  604  907  214  424  748  817  666 1592  521
2172  356  467 1583  882 2139 2182 1961  781  678 1425 1361 1473 1713 1761 1617
 370 1073 1304 1369 1092  453  798 1283  973  565 1315 1204 1796  846 1447 1143
 959 1275 1213 2085  742 1309 1479 1760  703 1727  872 1479  686 1698 1057  387
1252  904  668  443 1600  930 1052  776 1049  402  361 1119  578  406  618  581
1095  670  641 1152 1060  567  433  374  579  235  325 1802  331  217  665  862
 182  312  864  732  783 1456  608 2066  491  400 1466  744 2013 2082 1865  875
 552  400  182  820  721 1735  851  740  551 1551 1769 1159  613 2072 1300 1605
 807 1017 1251  818 1259 2596  826 1137 1255 1123  943 1359  188 1282  271 2300
 483 2540  609 1038 2099 1766 2699 2493 2266  264 1398  304  699  538 1335  454
 393  173 1198 1370  760  216 1692  919 1286  435  879  861  548  913 2198  483
 803 1181  731  627 1086  292  883  279 1906  178 2156  490  662 1699 1430 2300
2117 1888  138 1023  884  755 1612  749  690  476 1501 1654 1049  516 1995 1149
1580  739 1079 1161  815 1214 2485  780 1100 1347  985  916 1361  260 1171  328
2202  445 2385  665  966 1969 1729 2568 2333 2108  177 1327  177 1486  757  506
 609  981 1474  967  681 1552 1317  936  594  197  928  316  723 2203  500  604
 482 1104  455  630  641 1058  562 1857  528 2425  220  704 1845 1122 2405 2428
2204  738  945 1362  587  335  435  930 1358  819  504 1496 1153  927  428  341
 803  180  649 2119  343  521  652  939  340  649  533  918  451 1783  362 2290
 130  568 1727 1105 2301 2285 2059  595  853  891 1082 1199  726   96  583 1125
 653  563  947  986 1493  560 1183  813  882 1033  902 1763  642 1032 1131 1604
 463 1556  663 1298  947 1461  795  371  882  967  973  768 1472  588  252  308
 803  920  309  238 1252  569  940  165  863  414  454  552 1745  269  482 1188
 355  397  833  713  432  666 1453  410 1758  642  262 1260 1051 1858 1737 1508
 592  598  222  814 1094  510  235 1335  820  892  100  626  541  219  524 1897
  90  410  952  605  238  706  570  622  503 1581  257 1985  396  309 1453 1039
2043 1972 1744  514  661 1025 .1227  617   90 1525  835 1114  263  770  700  400
 740 2049  311  630 1087  630  459  924  405  739  360 1749  115 2055  428  492
1568 1256 2166 2026 1796  303  853  663  632  999  572  972  225  763  908  451
 767  293 1240  726  420 1111  862  617  443 1374  586 1299  887 1070 1633 1057
 547  999  252 1483 1681 1489 1326  236  610 1156  557  642  879 1000 1467  558
1178  780  831 1038  879 1726  700 1023 1082 1631  488 1579  586 1320  982 1463
 796  371  802  949 1021  826 1508  550  546  983  397  821  411 1023  180  651
 478 1438  476  485 1333  235  525  827 1022  123  973 1155  715 1475  902  273
 953  882 1550 1457 1240  898  396 1479  745 1105  240  831  645  442  723 1983
 316  623 1152  543  470  939  482  669  443 1690  205 1969  510  455 1492 1238
2091 1938 1709  354  813 1163  676 1264 1473  839 1326  847  801 1254  976 1643
1157 1169  983 1905  878 1836  346 1590 1286 1621 1034  689  503  995 1376 1239
1828  674 1183  725 1399  549 1004  869 1427  818  882 1716  214  902 1222 1210
 390 1184 1225  949 1239 1210  660  863 1207 1446 1197  969 1042  741  865  821
 644  790  388 1374  803  484  968 1056  665  318 1420  794 1341 1017 1137 1836
1056  679 1200  189 1645 1891 1704 1403  442  699  453  290  483 1809  107  384
1024  511  251  712  646  525  585 1499  330 1885  495  231 1356  999 1949 1872
1644  567  591  950  410  690 2147  594  590  326 1191  499  504  838 1098  758
1794  703 2439  414  751 1837 1011 2374 2455 2237  928  921  624  325 1356  480
 369 1241  413  473  680 1097  166 1038 1049  781 1497  905  238  925  702 1506
1506 1287  998  216  479 1941  188  350  736  792  161  547  632  745  552 1607
 375 2115  296  392 1547  959 2121 2114 1890  641  676 1480  435  129  949  708
 325  355 1081  492 1007 1137  779 1759  774  291 1148  516 1688 1765 1573 1038
 231 1829 1603 2339 1524 1780 1673 2421 1315 2394  357 2136  825 2237 1589  579
1204  347  959  940 2338 1266  320  919  605  154  623  652  580  582 1508  344
1950  429  242 1402  949 1986 1943 1717  603  582  872  699  197  358  957  529
 861 1263  660 1849  645  240 1250  631 1802 1867 1650  923  341 1511  815  669
1092 1397 1019 1982 1010 2706  695 1061 2069 1148 2594 2734 2520 1212 1176  697
1051 1018  290  985 1280  743 1427  956  466  987 1110 1584 1395 1166  861  626
 469  761  607  685 1446  472 1969  457  254 1393  823 1963 1975 1752  739  515
1171  847 1069 1316  919 2063  776  598 1434  507 1926 2101 1898 1187  548 1144
  63 2145  317 2445  426  875 1972 1584 2571 2408 2179  194 1231 1094 1036  836
1371 1008  354  833  828 1429 1369 1146 1021  352 2083  259 2412  345  811 1925
1507 2523 2380 2151  220 1163 1828 1005 1903 1272  504  849  653 1114 1019 2044
 932 2165  330  559 1668 1291 2264 2130 1906  268  917 2377 1723  636 1720  534
 145  290 2281 1531  667 1829 1235 2410 2367 2139  519  972 1162  792 1744 1724
1500  796  361 1087  600  701  550 1635  917 1490 1787 1614 1553  486  678  727
2435 1461  229 2238 1560 2010 1353 1157
```

Initializations and Optimal Point for TR48

	initial 1	initial 2	optimal
f(x)	-464816.	-638524.94	-638565.
1	0.	11.19	144.
2	0.	127.20	257.
3	0.	-129.70	0.
4	0.	344.50	483.
5	0.	-40.72	89.
6	0.	-295.30	-165.
7	0.	-202.30	-72.
8	0.	-382.30	-252.
9	0.	-217.70	-88.
10	0.	-307.70	-178.
11	0.	178.10	311.
12	0.	-4.36	126.
13	0.	-123.30	7.
14	0.	-265.30	-135.
15	0.	28.28	158.
16	0.	70.57	209.
17	0.	-31.81	101.
18	0.	-222.30	-92.
19	0.	96.19	229.
20	0.	-52.79	80.
21	0.	-34.71	95.
22	0.	-59.16	71.
23	0.	-373.70	-244.
24	0.	-28.35	102.
25	0.	-141.70	-12.
26	0.	2.28	132.
27	0.	198.50	337.
28	0.	-69.16	61.
29	0.	-26.35	104.
30	0.	-88.72	41.
31	0.	130.80	261.
32	0.	-12.35	118.
33	0.	-30.70	99.
34	0.	-376.30	-246.
35	0.	23.18	156.
36	0.	-400.30	-270.
37	0.	197.10	330.
38	0.	-260.30	-130.
39	0.	813.50	952.
40	0.	-191.70	-62.
41	0.	31.29	161.
42	0.	345.50	484.
43	0.	-7.72	122.
44	0.	335.50	474.
45	0.	947.50	1086.
46	0.	722.50	861.
47	0.	-300.30	-170.
48	0.	73.20	206.

This problem seems very difficult. Another problem, called A48, and simpler, consists in defining

$$s_i = d_i = 1 \qquad i = 1,\ldots,n \quad .$$

The optimal value for this problem is -9870.

BIBLIOGRAPHY

Agmon, S. (1954), The Relaxation Method for Linear Inequalities, *Canadian Journal of Mathematics*, 6, 382-392.

Aizerman, M.A., Braverman E.M., Rozonoer, L.I. (1964), The Probability Problem of Pattern Recognition Learning and the Method of Potential Functions, *Avtomatika i Telemekhanika*, 25, 1307-1323; *Automation and Remote Control*, 25, 1175-1190.

Aizerman, M.A., Braverman, E.M., Rozonoer, L.I. (1970), *Potential Functions Method in Machine Learning Theory* (in Russian), Nauka, Moscow.

Auslender, A. (1970), Recherche de Point de Selle d'une Fonction, *Cahiers du Centre d'Etudes de Recherche Operationnelle*, 12.

Auslender, A. (1971), Methodes Numeriques pour la Decomposition et la Minimisation de Fonctions Non-Differentiables, *Numerische Mathematik*, 18, 213-223.

Auslender, A. (1972), *Problemes de Minimax via l'Analyse Convexe et les Inegalites Variationnelles: Theorie et Algorithmes*, Lecture Notes in Economics and Mathematical Systems 77, Springer, Berlin.

Auslender, A. (1977), Programmation Convexe avec Erreurs: Methodes de Epsilon-Sous-Gradients, *C.R. Acad. Sc. Paris*, Serie A-B 284, 2, A109-A112.

Bakaiev, A.A. (1966), *Computers in the Planning of Transportation Networks* (in Russian), Technika, Kiev, USSR.

Bakaiev, A.A., Mikhalevich, V.C., Branovitskaia, S.V., Shor, N.Z. (1963), Methodology and Attempted Solution of Large Network Transportation Problems by Computer, in: *Mathematical Methods for Production Problems* (in Russian), Moscow.

Bakushinskii, A.B., Poljak, B.T. (1974), On the Solution of Variational Inequalities, *Doklady Akademii Nauk SSSR*, 219, 1038-1041; *Soviet Math. Dokl.*, 15 (1974), 1705-1710.

Bandler, J.W., Charalambous, C. (1974), Nonlinear Programming Using Minimax Techniques, *Journal of Optimization Theory and Applications*, 13, 607-619.

Bazaraa, M.S., Goode, J.F., Shetty, C.M. (1971), Optimality Criteria in Nonlinear Programming Without Differentiability, Operations Research, 19, 77-86.

Bazaraa, M.S., Goode, J.J. (1977), The Traveling Salesman Problem: A Duality Approach, Mathematical Programming, 13, 2, 221-237.

Bazhenov, L.G. (1972), On Convergence Conditions of a Minimization Method of Almost-Differentiable Functions, Kibernetika, 8, 4, 71-72; Cybernetics, 8, 4, 607-609.

Benders, G.F. (1962), Partitioning Procedures for Solving Mixed Variables Programming Problems, Numerische Mathematik, 4, 238-252.

Bertsekas, D.P. (1972), Stochastic Optimization Problems with Nondifferentialble Cost Functionals with an Application in Stochastic Programming, Proc. of the 1972 IEEE Conference on Decision and Control, IEEE, New York.

Bertsekas, D.P. (1973), Stochastic Optimization Problems with Nondifferentiable Cost Functionals, Journal of Optimization Theory and Applications, 12, 218-231.

Bertsekas, D.P. (1975), Nondifferentiable Optimization Via Approximation, in: Balinski, M.L., and Wolfe, P., eds., Nondifferentiable Optimization, Mathematical Programming Study 3, North-Holland, Amsterdam, 1-25.

Bertsekas, D.P. (1976), A New Algorithm for Solution of Nonlinear Resistive Networks Involving Diodes, IEEE Transactions on Circuit Theory, CAS 23, 599-608.

Bertsekas, D.P. (1976), Minimax Methods Based on Approximation, Proceedings of the 1976 Johns Hopkins Conference on Information Science and Systems, Baltimore, Maryland, 463-465.

Bertsekas, D.P. (1977), Approximation Procedures Based on the Method of Multipliers, Journal of Optimization Theory and Applications (to appear).

Bertsekas, D.P., Mitter, S.K. (1973), A Descent Numerical Method for Optimization Problems with Nondifferentiable Cost Functionals, SIAM Journal on Control, 11, 637-652.

Birzak, B., Pshenichnyi, B.N. (1966), On Some Problems of the Minimization of Unsmooth Functions, Kibernetika, 2, 6, 53-57; Cybernetics, 2, 6, 43-46.

Borwein, J.M (1976), Fractional Programming without Differentiability, Mathematical Programming, 11, 3, 283-290.

Bracken, J., McGill, J.T. (1973), Mathematical Programs with Optimization Problems in the Constraints, Operations Research, 21, 37-44.

Bracken, J., McGill, J.T. (1974), A Method for Solving Mathematical Programs with Nonlinear Programs in the Constraints, Operations Research, 22, 1097-1101.

Brondsted, A., Rockafellar, R.T. (1965), On the Subdifferentiability of Convex Functions, Proceedings of the American Mathematical Society, 16, 605-611.

Brooks, R., Geoffrion, A.M. (1966), Finding Everett's Lagrange Multipliers by Linear Programming, Operations Research, 14, 6, 1149-1153.

Butz, A. (1967), Iterative Saddle Point Techniques, SIAM Journal on Applied Mathematics, 15, 719-726.

Camerini, P.M., Fratta, L., Maffioli, F. (1975), On Improving Relaxation Methods by Modified Gradient Techniques, in: Balinski, M.L. and Wolfe, P., eds., Nondifferentiable Optimization, Mathematical Programming Study 3, North-Holland, Amsterdam, 26-34.

Cea, J., Glowinski, R. (1971), Minimisation des Fonctionnelles Non-Differentiables, Note 7105, IRIA, le Chesnay (France).

Charalambous, C. (1977), Nonlinear Least p-th Optimization and Nonlinear Programming, Mathematical Programming, 12, 2, 195-225.

Cheney, E.W., Goldstein, A.A. (1959), Newton's Method for Convex Programming and Chebyshev Approximation, Numerische Mathematik, 1, 1, 253-268.

Clarke, F.H. (1975), Generalized Gradients and Applications, Transactions of the American Mathematical Society, 205, 247-262.

Clarke, F.H. (1976), A New Approach to Lagrange Multipliers, Mathematics of Operations Research, 1, 2, 165-174.

Conn, A.R. (1973), Constrained Optimization using a Nondifferentiable Penalty Function, SIAM Journal on Numerical Analysis, 10, 760-784.

Conn, A.R. (1976), Linear Programming Via a Nondifferentiable Penalty Function, SIAM Journal on Numerical Analysis, 13, 1, 145-154.

Cordellier, F., Fiorot, J.Ch. (1978), On the Fermat-Weber Problem with Convex Cost Functions, Mathematical Programming (to appear).

Cornuejols, G., Fisher, M.L., Nemhauser, G.L. (1977), Location of Bank Accounts to Optimize Float: An Analytic Study of Exact and Approximate Algorithms, Management Science, 23, 8, 789-810.

Crowder, H.P. (1976), Computational Improvements for Subgradient Optimization, in: Symposia Mathematica XIX, Academic Press, London, 357-372.

Cullum, J., Donath, W.E., Wolfe, P. (1975), The Minimization of Certain Nondifferentiable Sums of Eigenvalues of Symmetric Matrices, in: Balinski, M.L., and Wolfe, P., eds., Nondifferentiable Optimization, Math. Prog. Study 3, North-Holland, Amsterdam, 35-55.

Dang Tran Dac (1973), Decomposition en Programmation Convexe, Revue d'Informatique et de Recherche Operationelle, R-1, 68-75.

Danskin, J.M. (1966), The Theory of Max-Min with Applications, SIAM Journal of Applied Mathematics, 14, 641-664.

Danskin, J.M. (1967), The Theory of Max-Min, Springer, New York.

Dantzig, G.B. (1960), General Convex Objective Forms, in: Karlin, S., Arrow, K.J., and Suppes, P., eds., Mathematical Methods in the Social Sciences, Stanford University Press, Stanford, California.

Dantzig, G.B. (1963), Linear Programming and Extensions, Princeton University Press, Princeton, N.J., chap. 24.

Dantzig, G.B., Wolfe, P. (1961), The Decomposition Algorithm for Linear Programming, Econometrica, 29, 767-778.

Demjanov, V.F. (1966), On Minimax Problems, Kibernetika, 2, 6, 58-66; Cybernetics, 2, 6, 47-53.

Demjanov, V.F. (1968), Algorithms for Some Minimax Problems, Journal of Computer and Systems Sciences, 2, 342-380.

Demjanov, V.F. (1970), Seeking a Minimax on a Bounded Set, Doklady Academii Nauk SSSR, 191, 1216-1219; Soviet Math. Doklady, 11 (1970), 517-521.

Demjanov, V.F. (1973), Second Order Directional Derivatives of a Function of the Maximum, Kibernetika, 9, 5, 67-69; Cybernetics, 9, 5, 797-800.

Demjanov, V.F. (1975), A Continuous Method for Solving Minimax Problems, Zurnal Vycislitel'noi Matematiki i Matematiceskoi Fiziki, 15, 592-598; USSR Computational Mathematics and Mathematical Physics, 15, 45-52.

Demjanov, V.F., Malozemov, V.N. (1971), The Theory of Non-linear Minimax Problems, Uspekhi Matematcheski Nauk, 26, 53-104 (in Russian).

Demjanov, V.F., Malozemov, V.N. (1974), Introduction to Minimax, John Wiley, New York.

Demjanov, V.F., Rubinov, A.M. (1968), Minimization of Functionals in Normed Spaces, SIAM Journal on Control, 6, 73-89.

Demjanov, V.F., Rubinov, A.M. (1970), Approximation Methods in Optimization Problems, American Elsevier, New York.

Dubovitskii, A.Y., Milyutin, A.A. (1963), Extremum Problems in the Presence of Constraints, Doklady Akademii Nauk SSSR, 149, 759-761; Soviet Math. Doklady, 4 (1963), 452-455.

Dubovitskii, A.Y., Milyutin, A.A. (1965), Extremum Problems in the Presence of Restrictions, Zurnal Vycislitel'noi Matematiki i Matematiceskoi Fiziki, 5, 395-453; USSR Computational Mathematics and Mathematical Physics, 5, 1-80.

Ekeland, I., Temam, R. (1974), Analyse Convexe et Problemes Variationnels, Dunod, Paris.

Elzinga, J., Moore, T.G. (1975), A Central Cutting Plane Algorithm for the Convex Programming Problem, Mathematical Programming, 8, 134-145.

Eremin, I.I. (1965), A Generalization of the Motzkin-Agmon Relaxation Method, Uspekhi Matematcheski Nauk, 20, 183-187 (in Russian).

Eremin, I.I. (1965), The Relaxation Method of Solving Systems of Inequalities with Convex Functions on the Left Side, Doklady Academii Nauk SSSR, 160, 994-996; Soviet Math. Doklady, 6 (1965), 219-221.

Ermolev, Yu.M. (1966), Methods of Solution of Nonlinear Extremal Problems, Kibernetika, 2, 4, 1-17; Cybernetics, 2, 4, 1-16.

Ermolev, Yu.M. (1969), On The Method of Generalized Stochastic Gradients and Stochastic Quasi-Fejer Sequences, Kibernetika, 5, 2, 73-84; Cybernetics, 5, 2, 208-220.

Ermolev, Yu.M. (1970), Stochastic Subgradient Methods and their Application (in Russian), Dissertation, Kiev.

Ermolev, Yu.M. (1972), On a Problem of Random Process Pro-
    grammed Control, Kibernetika, 8, 1, 79-81; Cybernetics, 8,
    1, 85-87.

Ermolev, Yu.M. (1975), Stochastic Models and Methods of Optim-
    ization , Kibernetika, 11, 4, 109-119; Cybernetics, 11, 4,
    630-641.

Ermolev, Yu.M. (1976), Stochastic Programming Methods (in
    Russian), Nauka, Moscow.

Ermolev, Yu.M., Ermoleva, L.G. (1973), The Method of
    Parametric Decomposition, Kibernetika, 9, 2, 66-69;
    Cybernetics, 9, 2, 262-266.

Ermolev, Yu.M., Marianovich, T.P. (1973), Optimization and
    Modeling, Problemy Kibernetiki, 27 (in Russian).

Ermolev, Yu.M., Nekrylova, Z.V. (1966), Some Methods of
    Sochastic Optimization, Kibernetika, 2, 6, 96-98;
    Cybernetics, 2, 6, 77-78.

Ermolev, Yu.M., Nurminskii, E.A. (1973), Limit Extremal Prob-
    lems, Kibernetika, 9, 4, 130-132; Cybernetics, 9, 4,
    691-693.

Ermolev, Yu.M., Shor, N.Z. (1967), On the Minimization of
    Non-Differentiable Functions, Kibernetika, 3, 1, 101-102;
    Cybnernetics, 3, 1, 72.

Ermolev, Yu.M., Shor, N.Z. (1968), Method of Random Walk for
    the Two-Stage Problem of Stochastic Programming and its
    Generalization, Kibernetika, 4, 1, 90-92; Cybernetics, 4,
    1, 59-60.

Evans, J.P., Gould, F.J. (1971), Application of the GLM Tech-
    nique to a Production Planning Problem, Naval Research
    Logistic Quarterly, 18, 1, 59-74.

Evans, J.P., Gould, F.J., Tolle, J.W. (1973), Exact Penalty
    Functions in Nonlinear Programming, Mathematical
    Programming, 4, 72-97.

Everett, H. III (1963), Generalized Lagrange Multiplier Method
    for Solving Problems of Optimum Allocation of Resources,
    Operations Research, 11, 399-417.

Falk, J.E. (1973), A Linear Max-Min Problem, Mathematical
    Programming, 5, 2, 169-188.

Feuer, A. (1974), An Implementable Mathematical Programming
    Algorithm for Admissible Fundamental Functions, Ph.D.
    Dissertation, Columbia University, New York.

Feuer, A. (1974), Minimizing Well-Behaved Functions, Proceedings of the 12th Allerton Conference on Circuit Theory, University of Illinois at Urbana-Champaign, Urbana, Illinois, 25-34.

Fisher, M.L. (1976), A Dual Algorithm for the One-Machine Scheduling Problem, Mathematical Programming, 11, 3, 229-251.

Fisher, M.L., Northup, W.D., Shapiro, J.F. (1975), Using Duality to Solve Discrete Optimization Problems: Theory and Computational Experience, in: Balinski, M.L., and Wolfe, P., eds., Nondifferentiable Optimization, Math. Prog. Study 3, North-Holland, Amsterdam, 56-94.

Fletcher, R. (1973), An Exact Penalty Function for Nonlinear Programming with Inequalities, Mathematical Programming, 5, 2, 129-150.

Fletcher, R. (1974), Methods Related to Lagrangian Functions, in: Gill, P.E., and Murray, W., eds., Numerical Methods for Constrained Optimization, Academic Press, London, chap. 8.

Fletcher, R. (1976), Conjugate Gradient Methods for Indefinite Systems, in: Watson, G.A., ed., Numerical Analysis, Dundee 1975, Springer, Berlin, 73-89.

Fletcher, R. (1976), Methods for Solving Nonlinear Constrained Optimization Problems, NA 16, University of Dundee Report, and in Proceedings of York State-of-the-Art Conference (to be published).

Gauvin, J., Tolle, J.W. (1977), Differential Stability in Nonlinear Programming, SIAM Journal on Control and Optimization, 15, 2, 294-311.

Gehner, K.R. (1971), Optimization with an Infinite Number of Constraints, and Application to Approximation Theory, Ph.D. Dissertation, University of Wisconsin, Madison.

Geoffrion, A.M. (1970), Elements of Large-Scale Mathematical Programming, in: Geoffrion, A.M., ed., Perspectives in Optimization, Addison-Wesley, Reading, Mass., chap. 2.

Geoffrion, A.M. (1970), Primal Resource Directive Approaches for Optimizing Nonlinear Decomposable Systems, Operations Research, 18, 3, 375-403.

Geoffrion, A.M. (1972), Generalized Benders Decomposition, Journal of Optimization Theory and Applications, 10, 4, 237-260.

Ghanem, M.Z.E. (1970), Optimal Control Problems with Nondifferentiable Cost Functionals, Ph.D. Dissertation, Stanford University, Stanford, Calif.

Gill, P.E., Murray, W. (1974), Newton-Type Methods for Linearly Constrained Optimization, in: Gill, P.E., and Murray, W., eds., Numerical Methods for Constrained Optimization, Academic Press, London, chap. II.

Goffin, J.L. (1971), On the Finite Convergence of the Relaxation Method for Solving Systems of Inequalities, ORC 71-36, Operations Research Center Report, University of California, Berkeley.

Goffin, J.L. (1977), On the Convergence Rates of Subgradient Optimization Methods, Mathematical Programming, 13, 3, 329-347.

Goldfeld, S.M., Quandt, R.E., Trotter, H.F. (1966), Maximization by Quadratic Hill Climbing, Econometrica, 34, 541-551.

Goldfeld, S.M., Quandt, R.E., Trotter, H.F. (1968), Maximization by Improved Quadratic Hill Climbing and Other Methods, Memo. No. 95, Econometric Research Program, Princeton University, Princeton, N.J.

Goldstein, A.A. (1975), Optimization with Corners, in: Non-Linear Programming 2, Academic Press, New York, 215-230.

Goldstein, A.A. (1977), Optimization of Lipschitz Continuous Functions, Mathematical Programming, 13, 1, 14-22.

Golshtein, E.G. (1970), Generalized Gradient Method for Finding Saddle Points, Ekonomika i Matematicheskie Metody, 8, 4 (in Russian).

Golub, G.H., Saunders, M.A. (1970), Linear Least Squares and Quadratic Programming, in: Abadie, J., ed., Integer and Nonlinear Programming, North-Holland, Amsterdam.

Greenberg, H.J. (1969), Lagrangian Duality Gaps: Their Source and Resolution, C.P. 69005, Technical Report, Southern Methodist University, Dallas, Texas.

Greenberg, H.J., Robbins, T.C. (1970), The Theory and Computation of Everett's Lagrange Multipliers by Generalized Linear Programming, C.P. 470008, Technical Report, Southern Methodist University, Dallas, Texas.

Grinold, R.C. (1970), Lagrangian Subgradients, Management Science, 17, 185-188.

Grinold, R.C.   (1972), Steepest Ascent for Large Scale Linear
    Programs, SIAM Review, 14, 447-464.

Gupal, A.M.   (1974), One Stochastic Programming Problem with
    Constraints of a Probabilistic Nature, Kibernetika, 10, 6,
    94-100; Cybernetics, 10, 6, 1019-1026.

Gupal, A.M.   (1977), On a Minimization Method for Almost-
    Differentiable Functions, Kibernetika, 13, 1, 114-116.

Gupal, A.M., Norkin, V.I.   (1977), A Minimization Algorithm for
    Discontinuous Functions, Kibernetika, 13, 2, 73-75.

Guseva, O.V.   (1971), Convergence Rate of the Method of Gen-
    eralized Stochastic Gradients, Kibernetika, 7, 4, 143-145;
    Cybernetics, 7, 4, 738-742.

Han, Shih-Ping   (1976), Superlinearly Convergent Variable
    Metric Algorithms for General Nonlinear Programming Prob-
    lems, Mathematical Programming, 11, 3, 263-282.

Heins, W., Mitter, S.K.   (1970), Conjugate Convex Functions,
    Duality and Optimal Control Problems, I: Systems Governed
    by Ordinary Differential Equations, Information Sciences,
    2, 211-243.

Held, M., Karp, R.M., Wolfe, P.   (1972), Large-Scale Optimiza-
    tion and the Relaxation Method, Proceedings of the 25th
    National ACM Meeting, held at Boston, Mass.

Held, M., Wolfe, P., Crowder, H.   (1974), Validation of Subgra-
    dient Optimization, Mathematical Programming, 6, 1, 62-88.

Hiriat-Yrruty, J.B.   (1978), On Optimality Conditions in Non-
    differentiable Programming, Mathematical Programming, 14
    (to appear).

Hogan, W.W.   (1973), Directional Derivatives for Extremal
    Valued Functions with Applications to the Completely Con-
    vex Case, Operations Research, 21, 1, 188-209.

Judin, D.B., Nemiroviskii, A.S.   (1976), Evaluation of Informa-
    tion Complexity for Mathematical Programming Problems,
    Ekonomika i Matematicheskie Metody, 12, 1, 128-142 (in
    Russian).

Judin, D.B., Nemirovskii, A.S.   (1976), Information Complexity
    and Effective Methods for Solving Convex Extremum Prob-
    lems, Ekonomika i Matematicheskie Metody, 12, 2, 357-369
    (in Russian).

Kantorovich, L.V., Akilov, K.P.   (1965), Functional Analysis in
    Normed Spaces, Pergamon Press, New York, chap. 15.

Kaplan, S. (1966), Solution of the Lorie-Savage and Similar Integer Programming Problems by the Generalized Lagrange Multiplier Method, Operations Research, 14, 1130-1136.

Karpinskaja, N.N. (1967), Methods of "Penalty" Functions and the Foundations of Pyne's Method, Avtomatika i Telemehanika, 28, 140-146; Automation and Remote Control, 28, 124-129.

Katkovnik, V.Ja. (1976), Linear Estimates and Stochastic Optimization Problems (in Russian), Nauka, Moscow.

Kelley, J.E. (1960), The Cutting Plane Method for Solving Convex Programs, Journal of the Society for Industrial and Applied Mathematics, 8, 4, 703-712.

Kennington, J., Shalaby, M. (1977), An Effective Subgradient Procedure for Minimal Cost Multicommodity Flow Problems, Management Science, 23, 9, 994-1004.

Korovin, S.K., Utkin, V.I. (1976), Method of Piecewise Smooth Penalty Functions, Avtomatika i Telemehanika, 37, 94-105; Automation and Remote Control, 37, 39-48.

Kupatadze, O.V. (1972), On the Gradient Method for Unsmooth Functions Minimization, Optimalnye i Adaptivnye Sistemy (in Russian), Trudy 4 Vsesojuzn. Sovesch. po Avt. Upr. (Tbilisi, 1968), Nauka, Moscow.

Kuzovkin, A.I., Tihomirov, V.M. (1967), On a Quantity of Observations for Finding a Minimum of a Convex Function, Ekonomika i Matematicheskie Metody, 3, 1, 95-103 (in Russian).

Lasdon, L.S. (1970), Optimization Theory for Large Systems, Macmillan, New York.

Laurent, P.J. (1972), Approximation et Optimisation, Hermann, Paris.

Laurent, R., Carasso, C. (1978), Un Algorithme de Minimisation en Chaine en Optimisation Convexe, SIAM Journal on Control and Optimization (to appear).

Lebourg, G. (1975), Valeur Moyenne pour Gradient Generalise, C.R. Acad. Sc. Paris, 281, 795-797.

Lemarechal, C. (1974), An Algorithm for Minimizing Convex Functions, in: Rosenfeld, J.L., ed., Information Processing '74, North-Holland, Amsterdam, 552-556.

Lemarechal, C. (1974), Minimization of Nondifferentiable Functions with Constraints, Proceedings of the 12th Allerton Conference on Circuit Theory, University of Illinois at Urbana-Champaign, Urbana, Illinois, 16-24.

Lemarechal, C. (1974), Note on an Extension of "Davidon" Methods to Nondifferentiable Functions, Mathematical Programming, 7, 3, 384-387.

Lemarechal, C. (1975), An Extension of Davidon Methods to Non-differentiable Problems, in: Balinski, M.L., and Wolfe, P., eds., Nondifferentiable Optimization, Mathematical Programming Study 3, North-Holland, Amsterdam, 95-109.

Lemarechal, C. (1975), Nondifferentiable Optimization; Subgradient and Epsilon-Subgradient Methods, in: Oettli, W., ed., Lecture Notes in Economics and Mathematical Systems No. 117, Springer, Berlin, 191-199.

Lemarechal, C. (1976), Combining Kelley's and Conjugate Gradient Methods, Abstracts, 9th International Symposium on Mathematical Programming, Budapest.

Lemarechal, C. (1978), Nonsmooth Optimization and Descent Methods, Research Report, International Institute for Applied Systems Analysis, Laxenburg, Austria (to appear).

Levin, A.Ju. (1965), On an Algorithm for the Minimization of Convex Functions, Doklady Academii Nauk SSSR, 160, 1244-1247; Soviet Math. Doklady, 6 (1965), 286-290.

Levitin, E.S. (1969), A General Minimization Method for Unsmooth Extremal Problems, Zurnal Vycislitel'noi Matematiki i Matematiceskoi Fiziki , 9, 783-806; USSR Computational Mathematics and Mathematical Physics, 9, 63-69.

Levitin, E.S., Poljak, B.T. (1966), Convergence of Minimizing Sequences in Conditional Extremum Problems, Doklady Akademii Nauk SSSR, 168, 993-996; Soviet Math. Doklady, 7 (1966), 764-767.

Litvakov, B.M. (1968), Convergence of Recurrent Algorithms for Pattern Recognition Learning, Avtomatica i Telemehanika, 29, 142-150; Automation and Remote Control, 29, 121-128.

Litvakov, B.M. (1973), On a Class of Robbins-Monro Procedures, Information Science, 6, 1.

Luenberger, D.G. (1970), Control Problems with Kinks, IEEE Transactions on Automatic Control, AC-15, 570-575.

Madsen, K. (1975), An Algorithm for Minimax Solution of Over-determined Systems of Nonlinear Equations, Journal Inst. Maths. Applics., 16, 321-328.

Madsen, K. (1975), Minimax Solution of Nonlinear Equations without Calculating Derivatives, in: Balinski, M.L., and Wolfe, P., eds., Nondifferentiable Optimization, Mathematical Programming Study 3, North-Holland, Amsterdam, 110-126.

Madsen, K., Schjaer-Jacobsen, H. (1978), Linearly Constrained Minimax Optimization, _Mathematical Programming_ (to appear).

Marsten, R.E. (1975), The Use of the Boxstep Method in Discrete Optimization, in: Balinski, M.L., and Wolfe, P., eds., _Nondifferentiable Optimization_, Mathematical Programming Study 3, North-Holland, Amsterdam, 127-144.

Marsten, R.E., Hogan, W.W., Blankenship, J.W. (1975), The Boxstep Method for Large-Scale Optimization, _Operations Research_, 23, 3, 389-405.

Maystrovsky, G.D. (1976), On Gradient Method of Saddle Points Searching, _Ekonomika i Matematicheski Metody_, 12, 5, 917-929 (in Russian).

Mifflin, R. (1976), _Semismooth and Semiconvex Functions in Constrained Optimization_, RR-76-21, International Institute for Applied Systems Analysis, Laxenburg, Austria [to appear in: _SIAM Journal on Control and Optimizaion_, 15, 6, 959-972].

Mifflin, R. (1977), An Algorithm for Constrained Optimization with Semismooth Functions, _Mathematics of Operations Research_, 2, 2, 191-207.

Mikhalevich, V.S., Ermolev, Yu.M., Skurba, V.V., Shor, N.Z. (1967), Complex Systems and Solution of Extremal Problems, _Kibernetika_, 3, 5, 29-39; _Cybernetics_, 3, 5, 25-34.

Minch, R.A. (1971), Applications of Symmetric Derivatives in Mathematical Programming, _Mathematical Programming_, 1, 307-321.

Moreau, J.J. (1963), Fonctionnelles Sous-Differentiables, _C.R. Acad. Sc. Paris_, 257, 4117-4119.

Moreau, J.J. (1965), Semi-Continuite de Sous-Gradient d'une Fonctionnelle, _C.R. Acad. Sc. Paris_, 260, 1067-1070.

Motzkin, T., Schoenberg, I.J. (1954), The Relaxation Method for Linear Inequalities, _Canadian Journal of Mathematics_, 6, 393-404.

Muckstadt, J.A., Koenig, S.A. (1977), An Application of Lagrangian Relaxation to Scheduling in Power-Generation Systems, _Operations Research_, 25, 3, 387-403.

Narula, S.C., Ogbu, U.I., Samuelsson, H.M. (1977), An Algorithm for the p-Median Problem, _Operations Research_, 25, 4, 709-713.

Nemhauser, G.L., Ullman, Z. (1968), A Note on the Generalized Lagrange Multiplier Solution to an Integer Programming Problem, Operations Research, 16, 2, 450-452.

Neustadt, L.W. (1963), The Existence of Optimal Controls in the Absence of Convexity Conditions, Journal of Mathematical Analysis and Applications, 7, 110-117.

Neustadt, L.W. (1969), A General Theory of Extremals, Journal of Computer and Systems Sciences, 3, 57-92.

Nevelson, M.B., Hasminskii, R.Z. (1972), Stochastic Approximation and Recurrent Estimation (in Russian), Nauka, Moscow.

Newman, D.J. (1965), Location of the Maximum on Unimodal Surfaces, Journal ACM, 12, No. 3.

Nurminskii, E.A. (1972), Convergence Conditions for Nonlinear Programming Algorithms, Kibernetika, 8, 6, 79-81; Cybernetics, 8, 6, 959-962.

Nurminskii, E.A. (1973), Convergence Conditions of Stochastic Programming Algorithms, Kibernetika, 9, 3, 84-87; Cybernetics, 9, 3, 464-468.

Nurminskii, E.A. (1973), The Quasigradient Method for the Solving of the Nonlinear Programming Problems, Kibernetika, 9, 1, 122-125 ; Cybernetics, 9, 1, 145-150.

Nurminskii, E.A. (1974), Minimization of Nondifferentiable Functions in the Presence of Noise, Kibernetika, 10, 4, 59-61; Cybernetics, 10, 4, 619-621.

Nurminskii, E.A. (1977), On the Continuity of Epsilon-Subdifferential Maps, Kibernetika, 13, 5, 148-149.

Nurminskii, E.A., Zhelikhovskii, A.A. (1974), Investigation of One Regulating Step in Quasi-Gradient Method for Minimizing Weakly Convex Functions, Kibernetika, 10, 6, 101-105; Cybernetics, 10, 6, 1027-1031.

Nurminskii, E.A., Zhelikhovskii, A.A. (1977), Epsilon-Quasigradient Method for Solving Nonsmooth Extremum Problems, Kibernetika, 13, 1, 109-115; Cybernetics, 13, 1, 109-114.

Parikh, S.C. (1976), Approximate Cutting Planes in Nonlinear Programming, Mathematical Programming, 11, 2, 194-198.

Pietrzykowski, T. (1969), An Exact Potential Method for Constrained Maxima, SIAM Journal of Numerical Analysis, 6, 217-238.

Poljak, B.T. (1967), A General Method of Solving Extremal
    Problems, Doklady Academii Nauk SSSR, 174, 1, 33-36;
    Soviet Math. Doklady, 8 (1967), 593-597.

Poljak, B.T. (1969), Minimization of Unsmooth Functionals,
    Zurnal Vycislitel'noi Mathematiki i Matematiceskoi Fiziki,
    9, 509-521; USSR Computational Mathematics and
    Mathematical Physics, 9, 14-29.

Poljak, B.T. (1974), Stochastic Regularized Algorithms, Suppl.
    to Preprints, Stochastic Control Symp. IFAC, (Budapest,
    Sep. 25-27, 1974) Budapest.

Poljak, B.T. (1976), Convergence and Convergence Rate of
    Iterative Stochastic Algorithms, I. General Case,
    Avtomatika i Telemehanika, 37, 12, 83-94; Automation and
    Remote Control, 37, 1858-1868.

Poljak, B.T. (1978), Nonlinear Programming Methods in the
    Presence of Noise, Mathematical Programming (to appear).

Poljak, B.T., Tsypkin, Ja.Z. (1973), Pseudogradient Adaptation
    and Training, Avtomatika i Telemehanika, 34, 45-68;
    Automation and Remote Control, 34, 377-397.

Poljak, R.A. (1971), On Best Convex Chebyshev Approximation,
    Doklady Akademii Nauk SSSR, 200, 538-540; Soviet Math.
    Doklady, 12 (1971), 1441-1444.

Powell, M.J.D. (1976), A View of Unconstrained Optimization,
    in: Dixon, E.C.W., ed., Optimization in Action, Academic
    Press, London, 117-152.

Pshenichnyi, B.N. (1965), Convex Programming in a Normalized
    Space, Kibernetika, 1, 5, 46-54; Cybernetics, 1, 5, 46-57.

Pshenichnyi, B.N. (1965), Dual Method in Extremum Problems,
    Kibernetika, 1, 3, 89-95; Cybernetics, 1, 3, 91-99.

Pshenichnyi, B.N. (1969), Necessary Conditions for an
    Extremum, Nauka, Moscow [Engl. translation Marcel Dekker,
    New York (1971)].

Pshenichnyi, B.N., Danilin, Yu.M. (1975), Numerical Methods
    for Extremum Problems (in Russian), Nauka, Moscow.

Reid, J.K. (1971), On the Method of Conjugate Gradients for
    the Solution of Large Sparse Systems of Linear Equations,
    in: Reid, J.K., ed., Large Sparse Sets of Linear
    Equations, Academic Press, London, chap. 16.

Rockafellar, R.T. (1970), Conjugate Convex Functions in Op-
    timal Control and the Calculus of Variations, Journal of
    Mathematical Analysis and Applications, 32, 174-222.

Rockafellar, R.T. (1970), Convex Analysis, Princeton Univ. Press, Priceton, N.J.

Sepilov, M.A. (1975), The Generalized Gradient Method for Convex Programming Problems, Ekonomika i Matematicheski Metody, 11, 4, 743-747 (in Russian).

Shapiro, J.F. (1971), Generalized Lagrange Multipliers in Integer Programming, Operations Research, 19, 1, 68-75.

Shor, N.Z. (1962), Application of the Gradient Method for the Solution of Network Transportation Problems (in Russian), Notes, Scientific Seminar on Theory and Application of Cybernetics and Operations Research, Acad. of Sciences, Kiev.

Shor, N.Z. (1964), On the Structure of Algorithms for the Numerical Solution of Problems of Optimal Planning and Design (in Russian), Dissertation, Kiev, USSR.

Shor, N.Z. (1967), Application of Generalized Gradient Descent in Block Programming, Kibernetika, 3, 3, 53-55; Cybernetics, 3, 3, 43-45.

Shor, N.Z. (1968), The Rate of Convergence of the Generalized Gradient Descent Method, Kibernetika, 4, 3, 98-99; Cybernetics, 4, 3, 79-80.

Shor, N.Z. (1969), Generalized Gradient Search, Transactions of the 1st Winter School on Mathematical Programming, held at Drogobich, Vol.3, Moscow (in Russian).

Shor, N.Z. (1970), Convergence Rate of the Gradient Descent Method with Dilation of the Space, Kibernetika, 6, 2, 80-85; Cybernetics, 6, 2, 102-108.

Shor, N.Z. (1970), Utilization of the Operation of Space Dilation in the Minimization of Convex Functions, Kibernetika, 6, 1, 6-12; Cybernetics, 6, 1, 7-15.

Shor, N.Z. (1972), A Class of Almost-Differentiable Functions and a Minimization Method for Functions of this Class, Kibernetika, 8, 4, 65-70; Cybernetics, 8, 4, 599-606.

Shor, N.Z. (1975), Convergence of a Gradient Method with Space Dilation in the Direction of the Difference between Two Successive Gradients, Kibernetika, 11, 4, 48-53; Cybernetics, 11, 4, 564-570.

Shor, N.Z. (1976), Generalized Gradient Methods for Non-Smooth Functions and Their Application to Mathematical Programming Problems, Ekonomika i Matematicheskie Metody, 12, 2, 332-356 (in Russian).

Shor, N.Z. (1977), Cut-off Method with Space Extension in Convex Programming Problems, Kibernetika, 13, 1, 94-96; Cybernetics, 13, 1, 94-96.

Shor, N.Z., Gamburd, P.R. (1971), Certain Questions Concerning the Convergence of the Generalized Gradient Method, Kibernetika, 7, 6, 82-84; Cybernetics, 7, 6, 1033-1036.

Shor, N.Z., Shabashova, L.P. (1972), Solution of Minimax Problems by the Generalized Gradient Method with Space Dilation, Kibernetika, 8, 1, 82-88; Cybernetics, 8, 1, 88-94.

Shor, N.Z., Shchepakin, M.B. (1968), Algorithms for Solving Two-Stage Stochastic Programming Problems, Kibernetika, 4, 3, 56-58; Cybernetics, 4, 3, 48-50.

Shor, N.Z., Zhurbenko, N.G. (1971), A Minimization Method Using Space Dilation in the Direction of the Difference of Two Successive Gradients, Kibernetika, 7, 3, 51-59; Cybernetics, 7, 3, 450-459.

Silverman, G.J. (1972), Primal Decomposition of Mathematical Programs by Resource Allocation, I. Basic Theory and a Direction Finding Procedure; II. Computational Algorithm with an Application to the Modular Design Problem, Operations Research, 20, 1, 58-93.

Skokov, V.A. (1974), Note on Minimization Methods Using Space Dilation, Kibernetika, 10, 4, 115-117; Cybernetics, 10, 4, 689-692.

Thibault, L. (1976), Quelques Proprietes des Sous-Differentiels de Fonctions Reelles Localement Lipschitziennes Definies sur un Espace de Banach Separable, C.R. Acad. Sc. Paris, 282, 10, 507-510.

Tsypkin, Ja.Z. (1968), Adaptation and Learning in Automatic Systems, Nauka, Moscow [Engl. translation Academic Press, New York (1971)].

Tsypkin, Ja.Z., Poljak, B.T. (1974), Attainable Accuracy of Adaptation Algorithms, Doklady Academii Nauk SSSR, 218, 3, 532-535.

Witsenhausen, H.S. (1968), A Minimax Control Problem for Sampled Linear Systems, IEEE Transactions on Automatic Control, AC-13, 5-21.

Witsenhausen, H.S. (1969), Minimax Control of Uncertain Systems, Electronic Systems Laboratory Report, Report ESL R-2-69, MIT, Cambridge, Mass.

Wolfe, P. (1970), Convergence Theory in Nonlinear Programming, in: Abadie, J., ed., Integer and Nonlinear Programming, North-Holland, Amsterdam, chap. 1.

Wolfe, P. (1974), Note on a Method of Conjugate Subgradients for Minimizing Nondifferentiable Functions, Mathematical Programming, 7, 3, 380-383.

Wolfe, P. (1975), A Method of Conjugate Subgradients for Minimizing Nondifferentiable Functions, in: Balinski, M.L., and Wolfe, P., eds., Nondifferentiable Optimization, Mathematical Programming Study 3, North-Holland, Amsterdam, 145-173.

Wolfe, P. (1976), Finding the Nearest Point in a Polytope, Mathematical Programming, 11, 2, 128-149.

Zangwill, W.I. (1967), Nonlinear Programming via Penalty Functions, Management Science, 13, 5, 344-358.

Zukhovitskii, S.I. (1956), On the Approximation of Real Functions in the Sense of Chebyshev, Uspekhi Matematiceskhi Nauk, 11, 125-159 (in Russian).

Zukhovitskii, S.I., Poljak, R.A. (1964), An Algorithm for Solving the Problem of Rational Chebyshev Approximation, Doklady Akademii Nauk SSSR, 159, 726-729; Soviet Math. Doklady, 5 (1964), 1574-1578.

Zukhovitskii, S.I., Poljak, R.A., Primak, M.E. (1963), An Algorithm for the Solution of the Problem of Convex Chebyshev Approximation, Doklady Akademii Nauk SSSR, 151, 27-30; Soviet Math. Doklady, 4 (1963), 901-904.

APPENDIX

LIST OF PARTICIPANTS

R. Fletcher
Department of Mathematics
The University of Dundee
Dundee DD1 4HN
UK

J. Gauvin
Départment de Mathématique
Ecole Polytechnique
Campus de l'Université Montréal
C.P. 6079, Succursale A
Montréal, Québec H3C 3A7
Canada

J.L. Goffin
Faculty of Management
McGill University
1001 Sherbrooke Street West
Montréal, Québec H3A 1G5
Canada

A.A. Goldstein
Department of Mathematics
University of Washington
Seattle, Washington 98195
USA

C. Lemarechal
International Institute
  for Applied Systems Analysis
2361 Laxenburg
Austria

and

Institut de Recherche en
  Informatique et Automatique
78150 Le Chesnay
France

R.E. Marsten
Sloan School of Management
Massachusetts Institute of Technology
50 Memorial Drive
Cambridge, Massachusetts 02139
USA

R. Mifflin
International Institute for
  Applied Systems Analysis
2361 Laxenburg
Austria

and

Department of Mathematics
Claremont Men's College
Claremont, California 91711
USA

B.T. Poljak
Institute of Control Sciences
Academy of Sciences of the USSR
81 Profsojuznaja
Moscow 117806
USSR

B.N. Pshenichnyi
Institute of Cybernetics
Ukrainian Academy of Sciences
Kiev 252207
USSR

P. Wolfe
IBM Watson Research Center
P.O. Box 218
Yorktown Heights, New York 10598
USA